The best of
Both Worlds
bringing two *fun*
groups of Americans to
Italy twice a year...

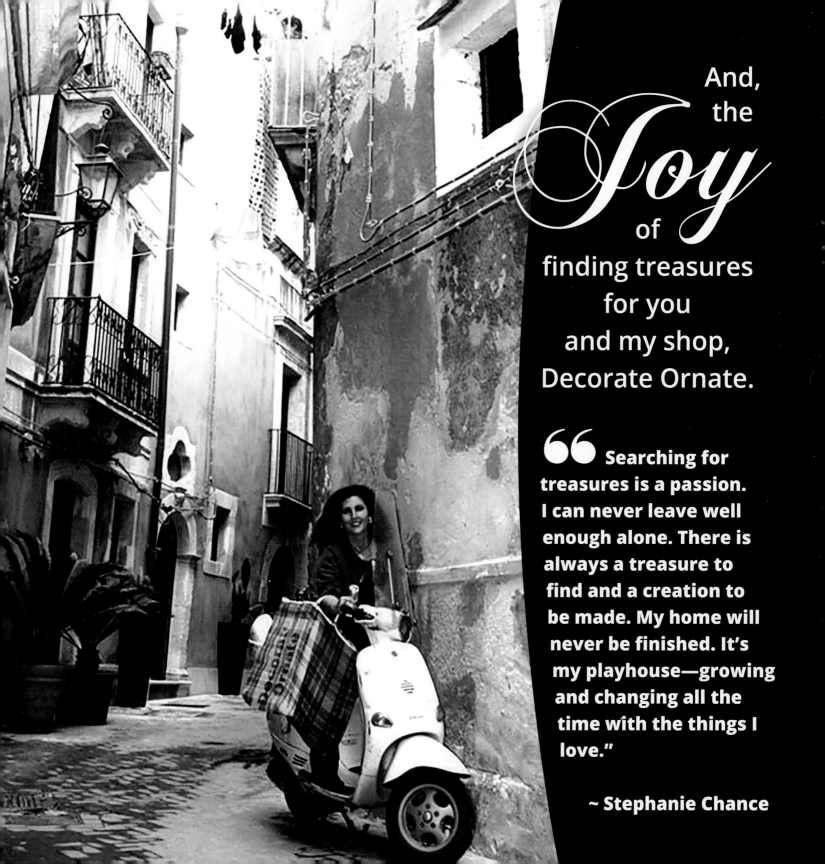

And,
the
Joy
of
finding treasures
for you
and my shop,
Decorate Ornate.

66 **Searching for
treasures is a passion.
I can never leave well
enough alone. There is
always a treasure to
find and a creation to
be made. My home will
never be finished. It's
my playhouse—growing
and changing all the
time with the things I
love."**

~ Stephanie Chance

Beautiful Seductions

From Italy to Decorate Ornate

Holiday Extravaganzas – Making All Things Beautiful

Adventurous Treasure Hunts in Italy

by Stephanie Chance

Publisher: Verona Valentino Editoria (Italy)

Photographer: Stephanie Chance &
Mindy Cowart Photography

Graphic Designer: Joni Guess

ISBN: 978-0-692-47923-0

Dedicated to:

My family
You give me the inspiration to decorate.

My loyal customers of Decorate Ornate
Thank you for allowing me to search the world for your home décor.

The Americans, fellow travelers of Decorate Ornate Italy Tours
My heart beats rapidly, anticipating our next magical adventure together. Thank you for giving me the joy of showing you God's amazing creations, inspiring you to make all things beautiful.

My granddoll, Kaitlyn Paige
Thank you for making my world so much fun. I hope you always live life to the fullest and never give up on your dreams. And, too, always make your home fabulously divine with the things you love.

Table
of Contents

I love to *Create Beauty* and bring magical seduction to a room.

" Your home should be the most beautiful place in the world, the place that reflects the King and Queen of the castle."

~ Stephanie Chance

Talking with Stephanie...

Since opening the doors of my shop Decorate Ornate, everyone wants to know my secrets. The truth is there are no secrets when it comes to decorating and making things happen. I simply follow my passion for the things I love—the things that speak to me, and the things that create an emotional bond and cause my adrenalin to explode.

The number one question asked of me is, "How did you go from a paralegal to an importing business owner and zigzagging all across Europe multiple times a year, and also leading Americans on exciting adventurous tours while writing a best-selling book *Mamma Mia, Americans "Invade" Italy!* How did you make all of this happen?"

The answer is simple—by taking risks—stepping out of the box of comfort while trusting and believing in God; listening to his inner voice and acting on it…and without a doubt, working hard, very hard. I still do. I take nothing for granted and thank God daily for his amazing grace and blessings. To make things happen, I truly believe you must act, take a step of faith, because faith without works is dead. We can sit all day and wish for things, but if we never 'get up' and actually do something, then it's time ticking away.

At a young age, I taught myself to crochet and then started sewing and making five-foot tall Raggedy Ann dolls—making their entire body, clothes and all, and even creating beautiful heads of curly red hair with yarn. I challenged myself with difficult sewing patterns; afterwards, I went on to create every fabulous cake I could find in cookbooks. I love to cook, especially baking. When my two children were small, I made and decorated cakes in all shapes and designs. The passion for baking, designing, and decorating has never left me; it has only blossomed, along with the adventurous side of me—the love of travel and searching for treasures. And as long as I can remember, I've had this unexplainable attachment to religious relics and fabrics—especially Damasks designs that originated in Damascus, Syria, and the heavy brocades of long ago.

> " Do what you love; do what God created you to do and you will love every single day of your life."
>
> ~ Stephanie Chance

It's true, aside from working in my shop Decorate Ornate, I do escape to Italy and beyond often, taking fun-loving Americans with me on magical adventures twice a year, and in between returning for buying trips. As you can see, I love working and making things happen. And when I do settle down in the late evenings with my husband, I curl up with my gigantic poodles and write—another passion burning within my soul.

When one enters Decorate Ornate, they start with the loud echoing out-bursts of oohs and ahhs from stepping inside a magical genie's bottle, captivating them into a fairy-tale world that expands from floor to ceiling with fabulous home décor of the most unusual kind. No more than a few steps within, I hear their words gushing. "Oh, I can just imagine your home. Do you have the same things in your home as in your shop?" they ask with wide-eye anticipation, reminding me of a small child seeing Saint Nicholas for the first time.

The truth is my home is my castle, my sanctuary, and my playhouse. It's filled with the things I love and the things I've found throughout my many journeys across the pond. The minute I walk into my home, I'm engulfed with beauty and that includes three black, Standard Poodles eagerly wagging their curly black tails, as they welcome me home in a wild, entertaining, and acrobatic kind of a way. Our furry, black canines reflect us, the Queen and King of the castle. I, along with my husband of twenty years, Allen Chance, grew up with poodles and have a tremendous love for them. They are a big part of our family and bring us so much joy. Our home reflects the love of our poodles, as well as of our family and friends. And when it comes to our furry canines, well, you will see that nothing is off limits to them and that includes red velvet chairs to genuine Italian leather.

I am blessed to have a husband that likes my taste even to the point of him being surrounded by colorful shades of pink bursting out in every direction. As you turn the pages of this book, you will see my love for flowers and the many shade variations of pink and red. You will see my love for decorating and surrounding myself with religious relics found throughout the many journeys to Europe.

After writing my first best-selling book *Mamma Mia, Americans "Invade" Italy,* I was bombarded with the question, "Stephanie, when will you write a book about you, a book showing us how you decorate your own home, a book that shows us how to use the vast collection of things we see in your Aladdin's cave-of-a-shop Decorate Ornate and more about your adventures?"

Well, this is the book you've been waiting for, and I'm delighted to share a glimpse into a few rooms of my home and inspire you to create and make 'your' holidays as fun and exciting as I do for my family. Each page gives you a peek into my home and family, along with the many journeys I take across the pond. I included a few selected homeowners who are faithful shoppers of Decorate Ornate and travelers on Decorate Ornate Italy Tours.

A man's home is his castle ...

Until the Queen Arrives

5

The Joy of Christmas

My home reflects me, not someone else. I'm often asked, "How do you have time to decorate your home, especially during the holidays, and still find time to operate Decorate Ornate, and also jet back and forth to Italy and beyond?" I answer with a smile,

> **When you love decorating and designing as much as I do, then it's a passion that burns within your soul. My home simply must be decorated."**
>
> ~ Stephanie Chance

When walking into my home, at first sight it appears as though I'm a devout Roman Catholic, pinching every sacred piece from the churches throughout Europe. The minute my extended papa, Tony Filaci, born and raised in Sicily and residing in the Italian Riviera, walks into my home, he ceremoniously crosses himself before the many Madonnas surrounding him. The truth is I am not Roman Catholic. I was raised Methodist but have a tremendous love and respect for the Roman Catholics. In fact, if you read my book, *Mamma Mia, Americans "Invade" Italy*, you'll know that I wanted to be a nun and live in my beloved Italy.

I simply adore the intricate hand-carved religious relics that shroud Europe and feel magnetized toward them. As I said earlier, there is an unexplainable, magnetic pull that draws me toward the many relics relating to the church—such as the long list of intricate Icons and Ex Votos in silver repousse, especially the Ex Votos with the letters GR on them, meaning 'grace received.' Also Madonna shrines, Syrian inlaid mother-of-pearl décor, Reliquaries, antique crowns, worn tapestries

portraying the days of Jesus, priest vestments, worn altars, carved columns with Corinthian capitals, gilded altar pieces, and my favorite, the Triptych of hand-painted saints which I have three in my home—all from Italy.

The biggest question of all—the one I'm asked to divulge, over and over, is, "Where do you find all of these amazing treasures for Decorate Ornate and your home—assuming your home is filled with them too?" I simple reply, "I zigzag throughout the rolling hills of Europe, searching for treasures."

Now that I've explained and hopefully answered your questions, come along with me and enjoy my home during the most magical time of the year, Christmas, our Lord and Savior's birthday, along with many other celebrations. Observe the photos carefully, and you will see the hidden treasures that I love so much, the things I've personally found throughout my many trips abroad. And, as you requested, I added a few of the photos of us searching and buying treasures while in Italy.

But first, I want to show you my entrance 'before' the Christmas décor magically transforms everything into a winter wonderland. As you see, the entrance is bare and naked because the Halloween décor was taken away minutes after the photo was snapped.

However, I must tell you about the empty, pink velvet chair. The chair was home to my beloved Humpty Dumpty. That is, until he literally had a great fall and, couldn't be put back together again. If you look closely throughout this book, you'll see him in some of the photos. Of course, it was before he had his great fall.

Since I never take away my treasures while decorating, you must look carefully to see them, because they are, at times, buried among the holiday décor. I go against my own education of interior design and break rules. Therefore, my home is truly my castle, not someone else's.

For instance, you know the rule—always place your table décor below eye level of your guest who is seated at the table. I wonder who made this rule. It doesn't really matter though, because like I said, I don't always follow someone else's rules. I decorate with the things I love and do whatever pleases me, not someone else. I fell in love with three tall compotes in Dresden, Germany, many years ago. Year after year, they stand tall on my dining room table and I never remove them; I only enhance them. Therefore, come along with me and hold on tight as you enter my world. I have limited my words so you can enjoy the photos and the many treasures collected throughout my lifetime.

As far as I'm concerned, the first step into your home should be fabulously decorated…to the point of causing a spontaneous reaction from your guest.

The very moment the door swings open I want to hear a loud, "Wow!" I'm talking about a hair-standing-up-shocking-to-the-eye kind of emotional excitement upon witnessing such a beautiful site.

Come along, step inside my foyer. However, you might be a little startled at the oversize mirror towering high above with hundreds of colorful flowers bursting out into an array of red and pink hues that will surely trigger you to inhale the spendid floral bouquet. If you look closely, really closely—below the antique gold mirror, you will see an antique reliquary—a shrine made to display holy relics of saints or something sacred. The reliquary rests on top of an inlaid Egyptian commode. The commode is filled with treasures—such as an antique silver cross and crown found in Arezzo, Italy, along with a mother-of-pearl Bible from Israel and an inlaid Bible from Italy. As soon as you step inside, you will not only see the entrance, but also the dining room.

66 **The very moment
the door swings open
I want to hear a loud,
'Wow!' I'm talking
about a hair-standing-
up shocking-to-the-
eye kind of emotional
excitement upon
witnessing such a
beautiful site."**

~ Stephanie Chance

13

Chiquita, our Toy Poodle, is welcoming guests as I continue to decorate.

66 Decorating is what I love to do. It's my passion, my heart and my excitement— making my home magical."
~ Stephanie Chance

The first Saturday
of every November
finds me bringing out
the brightly colored
balls, stringing them
one ball at a time and
then, going from room
to room, decorating with
all of my collectibles.
Weeks later, when
my family and friends
arrive excitedly ringing
the doorbell, they
eagerly anticipate the
moment when the door
swings open and the
magical seduction of
Christmas magnetizes
them, instantaneously
slapping them right
in the face with the
dazzling allurement of
a guaranteed fairy-tale
adventure.

17

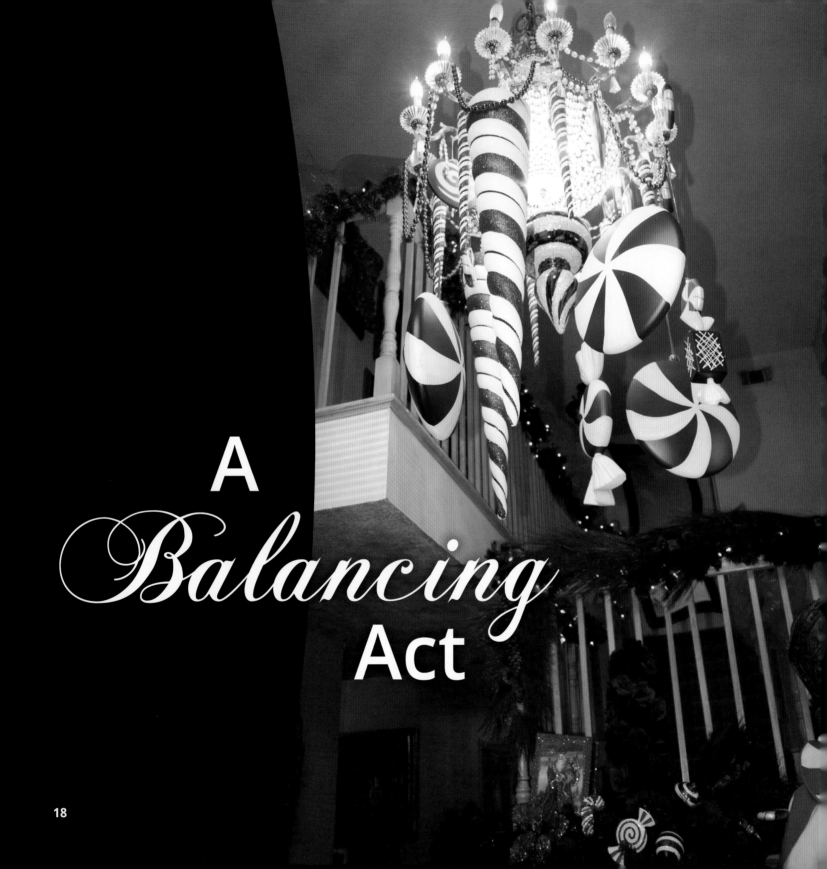

A
Balancing
Act

After attaching the lighted garland to the two-story stairway, I come back with 'real' pine sprigs and completely conceal the wood banister. While decorating, I nonchalantly placed the large red bow on the corner of the rail for lack of a better place to put it at that particular moment. Later, it went on a Christmas package. I love balance and would never use just one red bow on the railing. That is one rule I do agree with...it must have two for balance, but this Christmas it has none.

Remember
your
Guests

I love to give chocolates,
wrapped pretty and tied
with a bow.

My

Grandmother

always said,

" For goodness sake, if you can't be a work of art, then wear a work of art."

Oh, how my grandmother loved beautiful clothes; she was a manicured lady.

Many of my customers are intimidated by entertaining, dreading the potential judgment from their guests for not hiring a professional interior designer…or hiring a professional and afterwards, not being satisfied with what the decorator used in their home. This drives me crazy. I want to shout out, "Decorate your home with the things you truly love, enjoy your home with your friends and family, and if you need help, then get help but please, surround yourself with the things that reflect 'you,' not someone else. Buy what truly makes your heart happy, the décor that draws you to it. Who says you have to decorate according to someone else's likes? I certainly do not. I create my castle with the things I love; therefore, I love my home, and it reflects me, the Queen of the castle, not someone else.

> **" I love decadent details…blue painted sky ceilings are necessary in my home. I want to look up at the ceiling and get lost in the heavens while thinking; surely angels are flying above in the white, puffy clouds.**
>
> **~ Stephanie Chance**

The *Table*

is missing something, such as the plates, glasses, and candy-striped napkins.

Breaking Rules

... three, tall compotes from Dresden, Germany—

all filled with dazzling glass balls. My table is inspired by the intricate Dresden compotes—bursting with color. I work off them and the chosen fabric, which ignites my inner excitement beyond the normal behavior of just decorating a table. I could never leave a table naked and bare...no, never. And as I mentioned earlier, I broke the rule of keeping the décor below eye level around the table. Why? Because I love creating drama, mystery and seduction as we eat...and, I love it!

> "**God Created** each one of us as unique individuals; therefore, decorate with your own originality."
>
> ~ Stephanie Chance

Let visions
of
Fairy Tales
dance in their heads.

28

Our chandelier came from the famous Beverly Hills Hotel in California during its renovation many years ago. You might say it's a family heirloom.

The *Dining Room*

... is beginning to look a lot like Willy Wonka's chocolate factory of sugary delights. It's an explosion of colors mixed in with beloved treasures.

The *Moment*

one walks into my home,
the magical excitement starts.
I love gigantic, colorful bows
on the gifts.

32

Divine Style

... I love angels, and every home needs bronze—a forever heirloom. When searching for treasures in Parma, Italy, I found this beautiful, bronze angel.

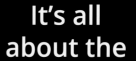

It's all
about the

First
Impression

Coming through the front
wooden door into a large
open foyer, expected
friends arrive in a large
open foyer overflowing
with curiosity and
anticipation; heads turn
and eyes flash in all
directions as they slowly
move toward the dining
room to the right. They
gawk at the massive
eruption of color twinkling
before their eyes, and
then slowly move toward
the table.

THE
LEGEND
OF
SAINT
Nícholas

35

> **66** The foyer—
> the entrance, is
> more than a pass
> through, it's the first
> impression people
> have of you and
> your home—make it
> fabulous."
> ~ Stephanie Chance

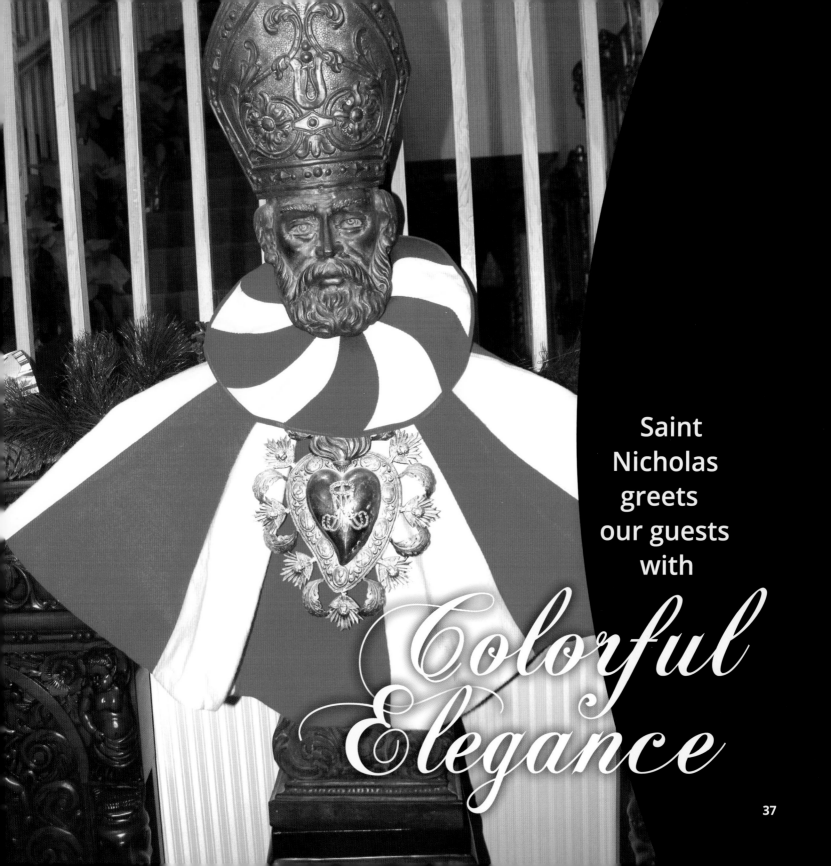

Saint Nicholas greets our guests with

Colorful Elegance

After the lighted *Garland* is attached, I add many pine branches to cover the entire railing.

A few years back, I found this antique statue of Saint Nicholas in Parma, Italy, and the Ex-Voto in Napoli, Italy.

Hmm...

Inspiration

comes from the strangest things. When I saw this teapot, the wheels started rolling within my head. I saw a beautifully decorated Christmas table with puffy, black and white harlequin fabric and red-glittered overlay, abounding with gigantic lollipops.

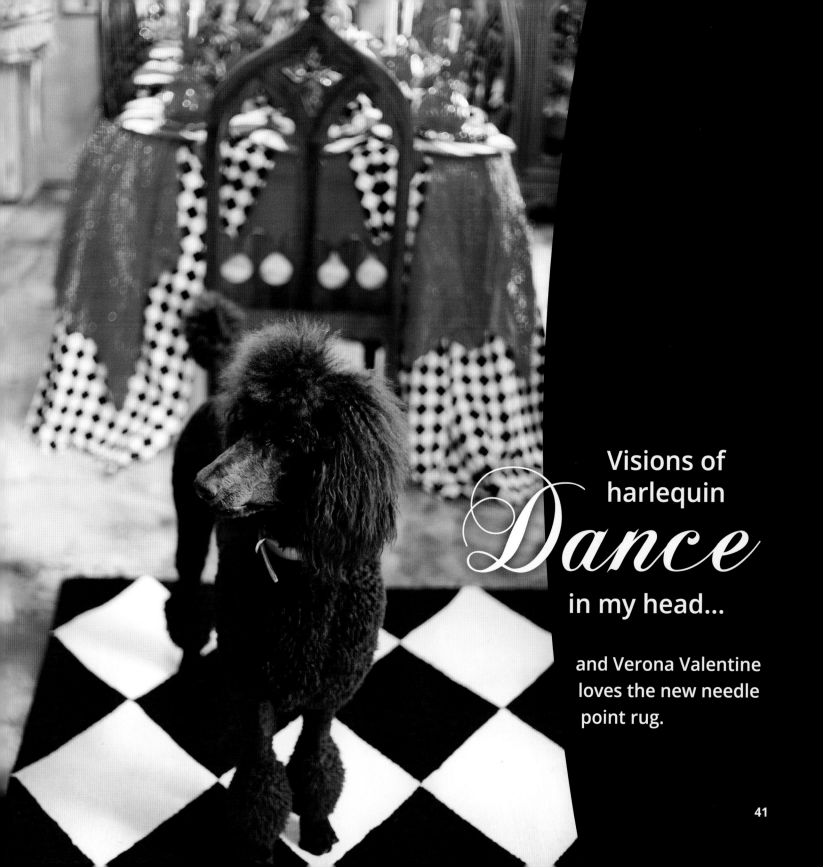

Visions of harlequin *Dance* in my head...

and Verona Valentine loves the new needle point rug.

41

Afterwards, I found this harlequin box, which compliments the snowballing imagines within my mind.

After moving Saint Nicholas a few feet back and placing huge red and green lollipops all around the table, along with making a ruffled harlequin cover around the chandelier, I stand with folded arms, approving the

Beginnings

of a harlequin kind of Christmas.

Harlequin

wrapping paper goes perfectly with my décor' this year.

Dim the Lights

... it changes the mood.

And the *Mistletoe* was hung with a bow on top.

It's a *White Christmas* ... but it's only the beginning.

Without

Memories,

we have nothing.

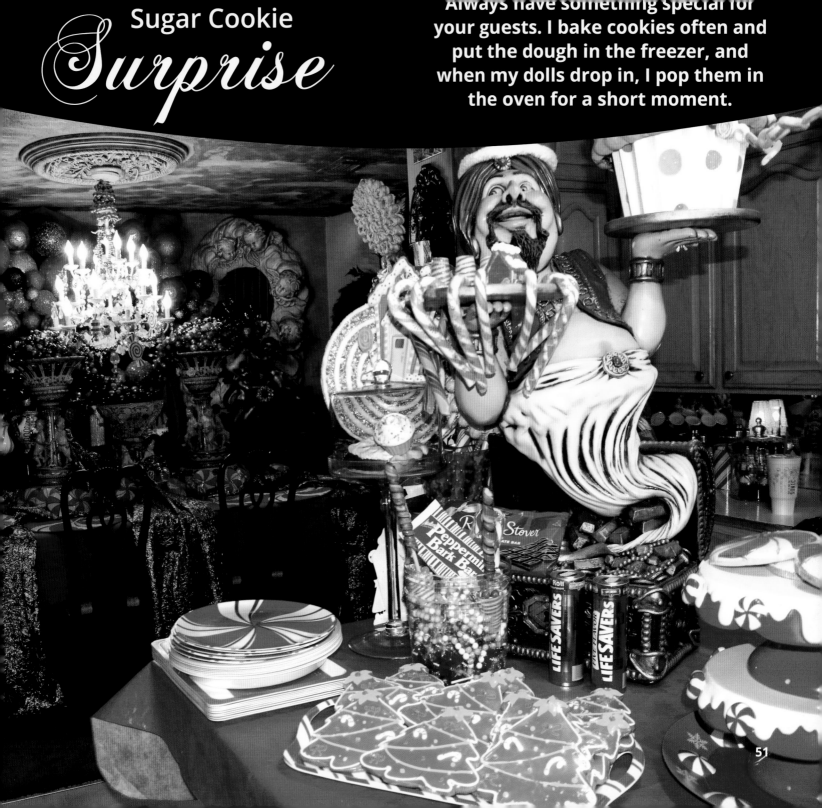

Sugar Cookie *Surprise*

Always have something special for your guests. I bake cookies often and put the dough in the freezer, and when my dolls drop in, I pop them in the oven for a short moment.

51

Blue Velvet
this year...

The green glow of *Stained Glass*

... found in the local market of Italy and now in my home—estimated to be over two hundred years old.

54

Fit
for a
Queen

Kaitlyn has grown up
with this gigantic chair
from Europe, and every
Christmas we decorate
it, adding a few more
things each year.

It's
all about
the
Bow

...and yes, I make my
own. It's really quite easy
and adds so much to the
presentation.

Touches of
Harlequin

**and for Kaitlyn's
love, touches of Zebra
with a red-striped big
bow...**

The *Excitement*

of gifts wrapped with a beautiful bow is priceless. And since I used harlequin fabric on the dining room table, I added a few touches of harlequin throughout the home.

Antique Shrine

—perfect for the Christmas story
books. And the love of frames...

Every Christmas brings new *Exitement* of decorating with the things I love.

I never take away my treasures, I add to them. The photos I'm sharing with you are not staged. Therefore, you will see Kaitlyn's overnight bags and everyday life of things around.

Mother Teresa

creates an awesome Christmas skirt made of craft paper.

When it comes to decorating, cooking and creating the most fabulous things, Teresa Chance wins the prize of creativity. She is blessed with a plethora of talents that always seems to amaze me.

It all started with a *Cupcake...*

Every year my dear friend, Jacque Gibbs, decorates her fabulous East Texas home into a winter wonderland. This year, Jacque purchased the gigantic cupcake from Decorate Ornate and decorated her dining room tree as an explosion of peppermint delight.

Prayer Room & Library

Every home needs a prayer room, and I must have a library because... I love to read. Come along and see the many religious relics inside my favorite room. However, I must warn you, it's a bit overwhelming and shocking to the eyes when you enter within.

71

The *Reliquary*

on the right side of the mantel is filled with Ex-Votos and so much more. And if you look closely, you'll see the wooden podium underneath the reliquary. On the glass coffee table is a beautiful hand-carved Florentine tray from Florence, Italy.

Inside

the reliquary: Ex-Votos,
Madonna crown, olive
wood nativity from Israel,
and so much more...

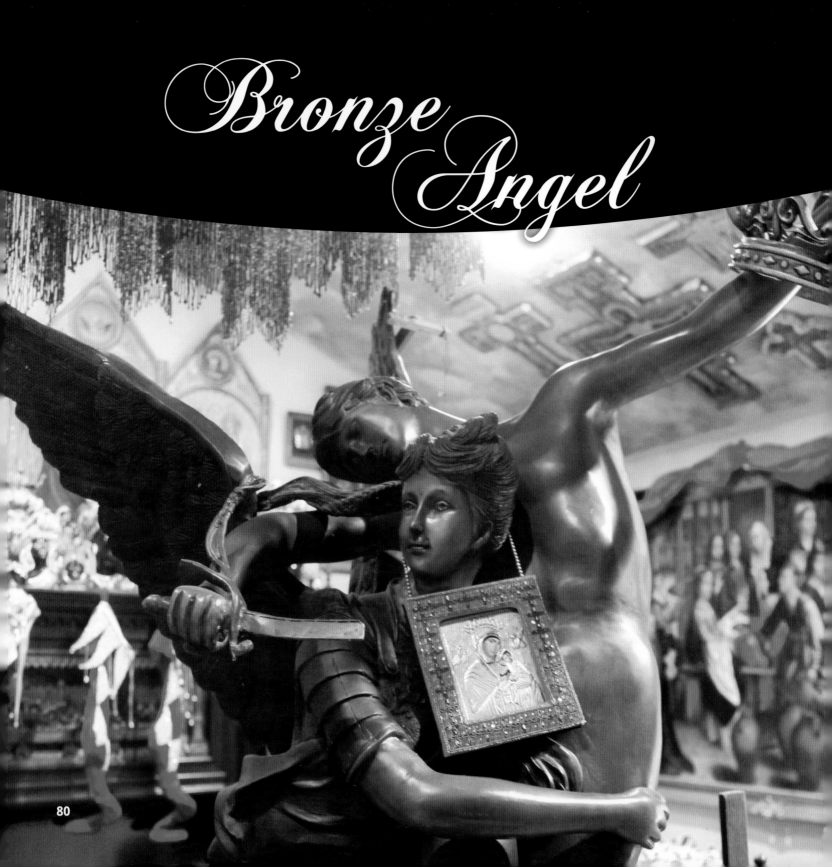

Bronze Angel

Capodimonte
Nativity
Set

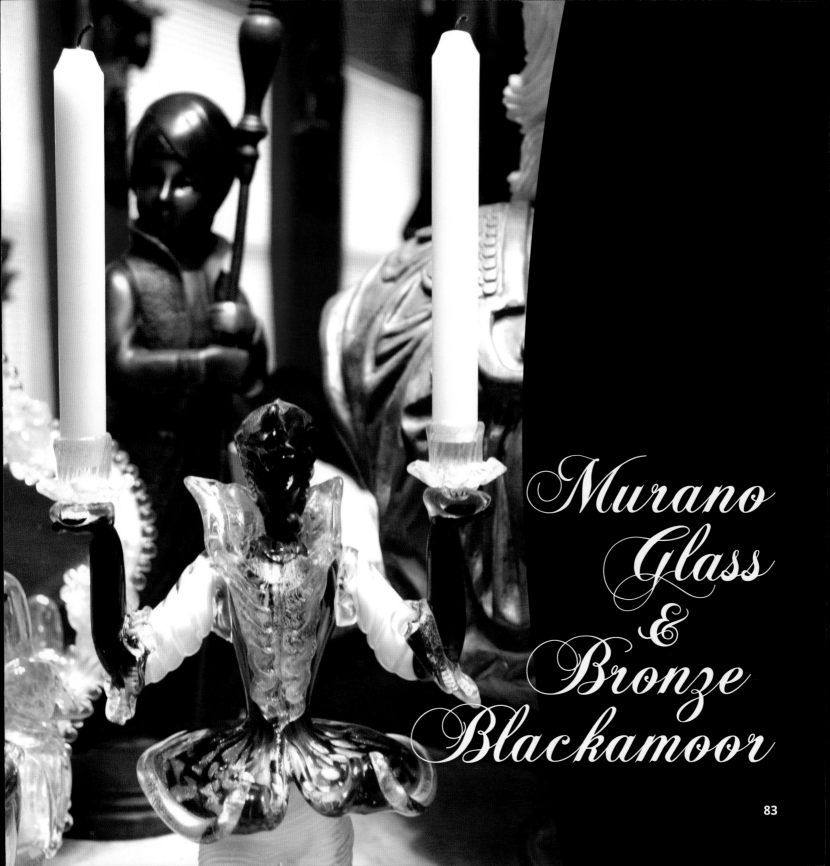

Murano Glass & Bronze Blackamoor

Reliquary filled with

Treasures...

and my love, the inlaid mother-of-pearl Bible, along with the Last Supper from Israel, the turtle from Sicily, and hand-carved cameos from the Mediterranean, all inside another antique reliquary.

Along with the towering, bronze statue and camel,
the two colorful Blackamoors (to the right) stand proudly ready to serve
their guests. Only in Sicily will you find the artisans who make these

Beautiful Creations

Lighting
the
Prayer Candle

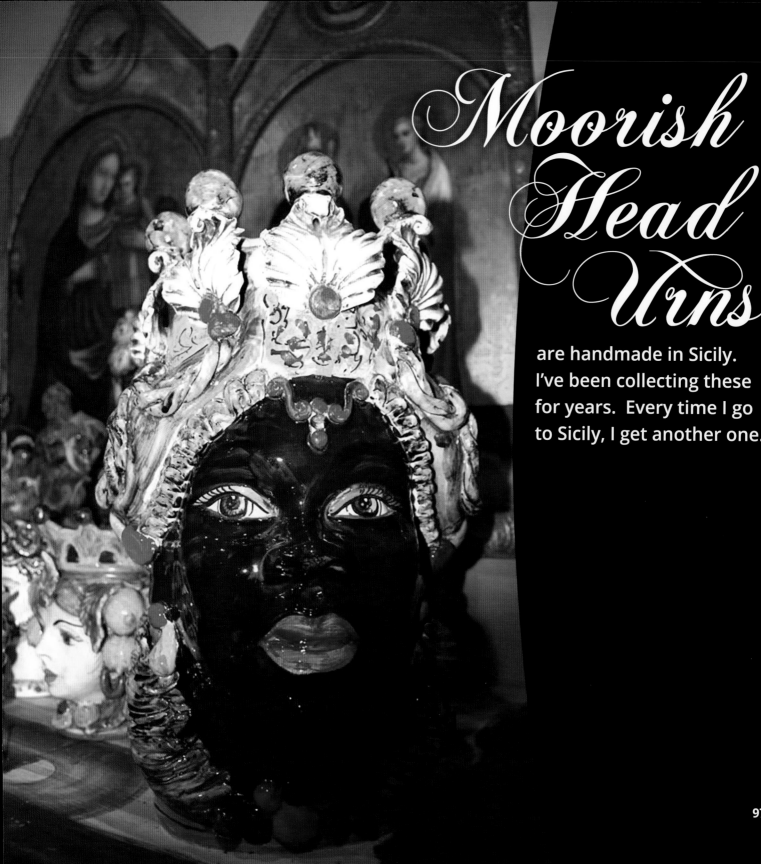

Moorish Head Urns

are handmade in Sicily. I've been collecting these for years. Every time I go to Sicily, I get another one.

The Triptych & Sicilian

Moorish heads... love them.

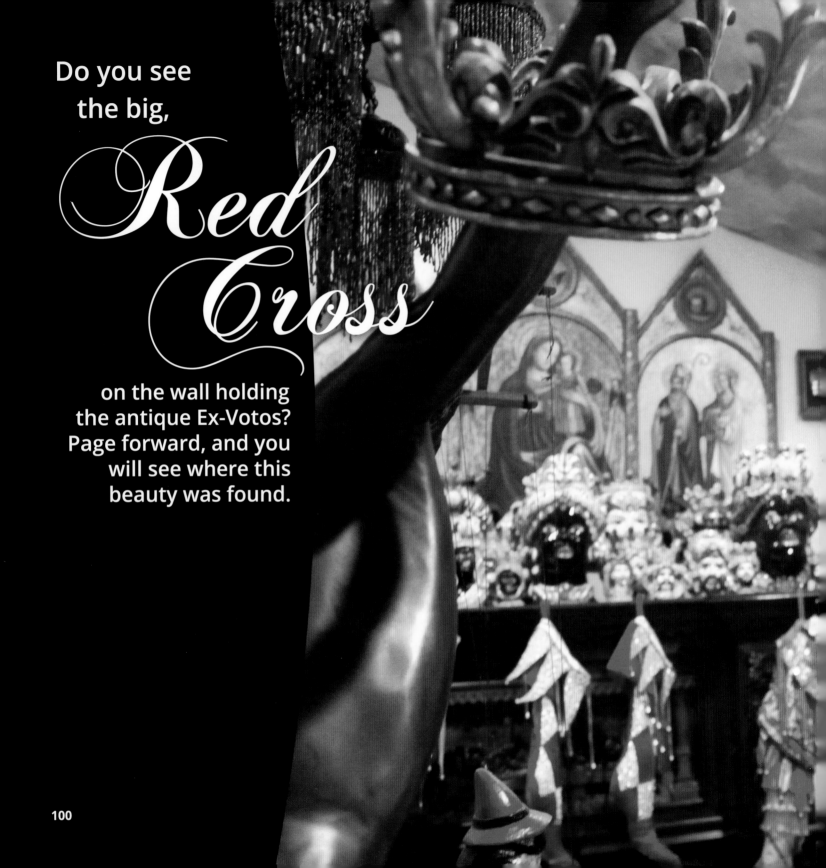

Do you see the big,

Red Cross

on the wall holding the antique Ex-Votos? Page forward, and you will see where this beauty was found.

100

Peppermint crochet *Afghan* makes its debut.

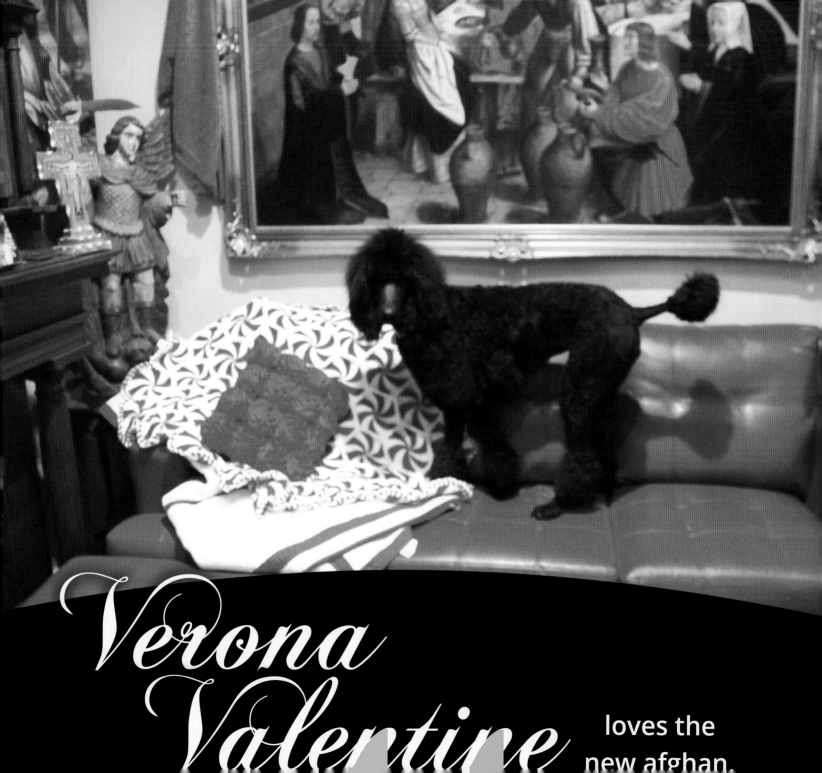

Verona Valentine

loves the new afghan.

I was
drawn to the
red and white

Peppermint

pattern
several years ago and
now it has snowballed into
many collectables. One in
particular is this handmade
crochet afghan by Alfred
Boedeker, a popular
designer in Austin, Texas.
His crochet talents are
truly amazing. And to my
surprise, Alfred shipped
me the matching pillow
and hat.

Peppermint
Delight!
Thank you,
Alfred Boedeker!

66 For goodness sak
if you can't be a piece
of art, then by all
means, wear a piece of
art!" my grandmother,
Fluff, repeated, as she
squeezed my cheeks,
encouraging me to hav
fun with her fabulous
hats and oversized
shoes.

~ Kaitlyn Paig

The Bedroom

... make it seductive and beautiful.

113

Until Death

do us part...

a reminder of what we'll be. In Italy, it's a very special day. One of the most bizarre celebrations of all...the Day of the Dead. The official day the Italians visit the dead as though they are still alive in the tombs. It's a celebration of love and remembrance of their loved ones. The day you see the locals toting armfuls of chrysanthemums along with the wax candles. Read about it in Chapter 10 of my book, *Mamma Mia, Americans "Invade" Italy!*

Southern Italy

Cemeteries

in Italy are fascinating, and my favorite one sits majestically on top of the Amalfi mountainside overlooking the beautiful turquoise sea and surrounded by Italian Cypress trees. I take these photos two and three times a year.

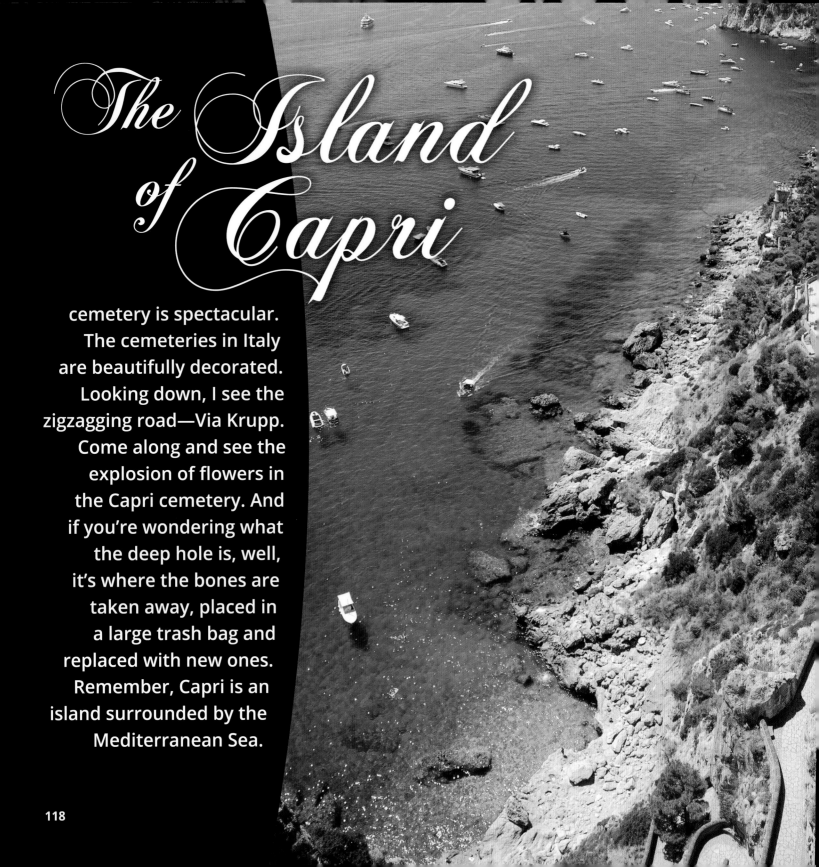

The Island of Capri

cemetery is spectacular. The cemeteries in Italy are beautifully decorated. Looking down, I see the zigzagging road—Via Krupp. Come along and see the explosion of flowers in the Capri cemetery. And if you're wondering what the deep hole is, well, it's where the bones are taken away, placed in a large trash bag and replaced with new ones. Remember, Capri is an island surrounded by the Mediterranean Sea.

Decorate
Ornate
www.DecorateOrnate.com

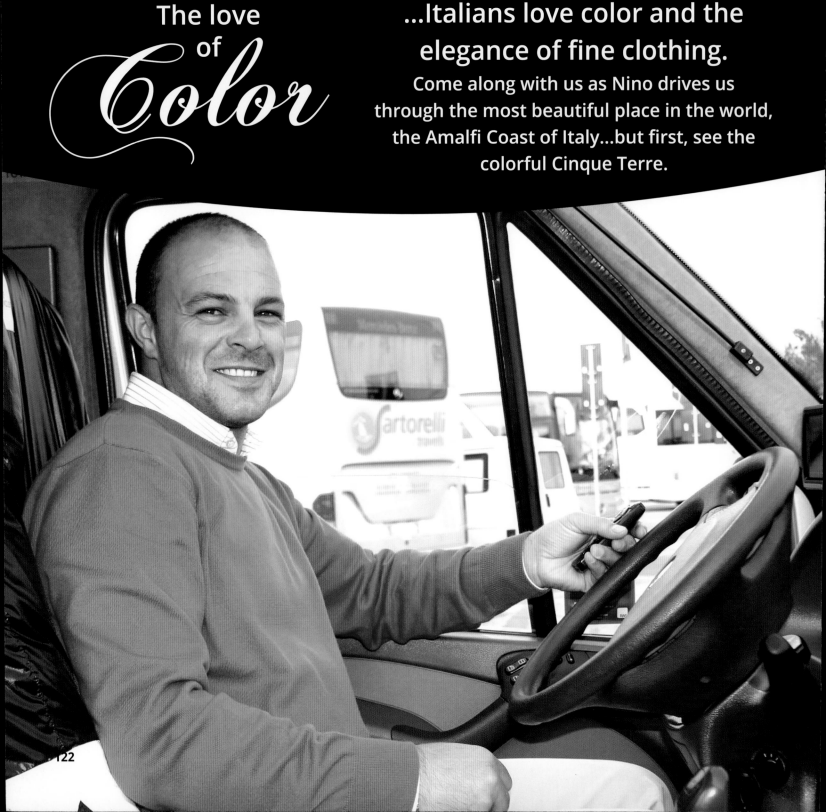

The love of *Color*

...Italians love color and the elegance of fine clothing. Come along with us as Nino drives us through the most beautiful place in the world, the Amalfi Coast of Italy...but first, see the colorful Cinque Terre.

The *Cinque Terre,*

the Italian Riviera....ah, it's truly a fairy-tale journey!

Hop aboard with us every year to the magical villages.

Reliquaries...

they come in all
shapes & sizes.

124

Tony Filaci

is friends to many and loved by all... beside him is another fabulous find...a black turtle, handmade by the locals in Sicily. This unique turtle is made from the volcanic ash from the largest volcano in Europe—Mount Etna—and is inlaid with the beautiful Abalone shells from the Mediterranean Sea.

Cameos

are hand-carved in Sorrento, Italy from the beautiful shells out of the Mediterranean. I love collecting them.

Nino drives us through the most beautiful place in the world, the

Amalfi Coast

With every twist and turn, we shout with excitement. The Americans on board right now are getting overly excited as we near, closer and closer, to our paradise home tonight. It's not here in Amalfi we anticipate, it's in Sorrento. Arriving at **Villa Giovanna** means we're immediately surrounded by friends and family who will pamper us with sinful Italian delights, not to mention our favorite restaurant, **La Tavola Di Lucullo**, both situated in Sorrento, Italy. See page 134.

The *Honeymoon Villa*

in Amalfi, Italy.

I snap this photo once again. We are in the breathtaking Mediterranean Sea in our private boat. Me, along with sixteen Americans stare at the fairy-tale beauty before us. Come on, hop aboard with us... twice a year. The memories will last you a lifetime.

Decorating...
the
Beauty
of the boat.

Here in Positano, Italy, locals name their boats, as well as their homes. It has nothing to do with size or grandeur; it's just a fun custom in Europe. My home is named Villa Barboncini, which means the house of poodles. I love the idea of naming my home because it adds a personal touch. Be creative, add a little sign with your castle name and hang it by the front door. Your home is your castle and don't forget, you are the Queen and King of your castle! Therefore, don't let it stop at the door, you can engrave your towels, napkins, letterhead...and so forth.

Decorate
Ornate
www.DecorateOrnate.com

Decorate
Ornate
www.DecorateOrnate.com

Texan in the Mediterranean Sea...
but the boots are safe and dry. Hop aboard with us to Italy and beyond, twice a year!

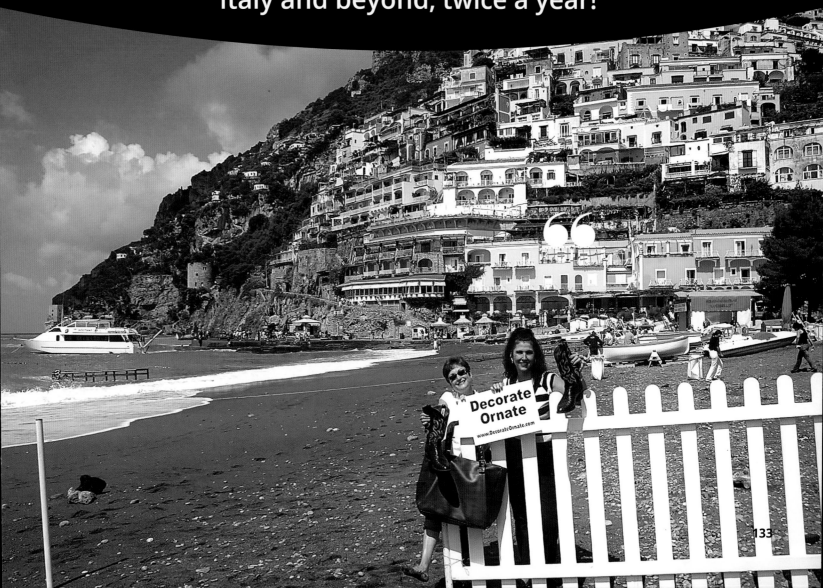

Decorate Ornate

www.DecorateOrnate.com

133

La Tavola Di Lucullo

restaurant in Sorrento, Italy

Prepare yourself for the most spectacular meal of all, and did I mention the pizza? Enjoy the 'daily' catch from the Mediterranean and the most beautifully decorated foods of all...our favorite.

Great Finds

this morning at the local market in Italy.

People say to me, "I can't imagine how you spent your entire career as a paralegal, working in the long box on countless court cases, right beside one of the most talented attorneys in East Texas. Then, in a moment's notice, you're traveling all over Europe, searching for castle doors and rare relics for your very own import store you named Decorate Ornate."

135

Being here in Arezzo, Italy, I spot the red

Velvet Cross

resting on the wall behind Allen.

It was love at first sight. Looking at it more closely, I knew it was from a church, but the Ex-Votos were missing. Pages back, you saw my personal prayer room/library and this red velvet cross, which is now filled with antique Ex-Votos.

Tony Filaci

is everything you have ever thought of when thinking of Italy. He's the spicy Italian-Romeo kind of man who's full of life and laughter. He's a sizzling slice of mozzarella cheese, stretched wide and flavorful over the beautiful regions of Italy while firmly caressing the beautiful body of his beloved homeland, Sicily. He's my best friend, always advising me before I make the big purchase.

Tony agrees...the wood frame is Florentine.

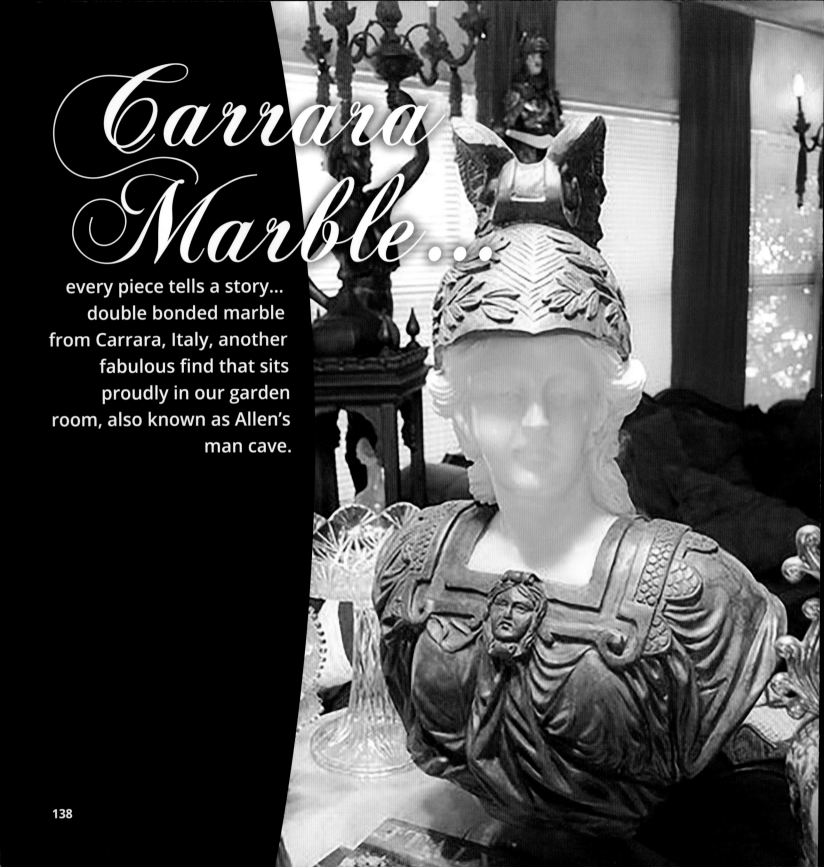

Carrara Marble...

every piece tells a story...
double bonded marble
from Carrara, Italy, another
fabulous find that sits
proudly in our garden
room, also known as Allen's
man cave.

Sicily...

taking two, fun groups of Americans to Italy, and beyond, twice a year—come on, hop aboard with us!

**Decorate
Ornate**

Our Fairy Tale Place

This is where we stay when visiting Taormina, Sicily.

Hop aboard with us, twice a year to Italy!

145

Hop aboard with us,
twice a year, and
Experience Italy
with the locals.

146

We're here
in
Sicily...

searching
for treasures for
Decorate Ornate.

Treasures from Europe **can ignite the imagination!**

Italian

Ceramic Tiles...

found in Italy and installed in these beautiful East Texas homes. Peggy Garmon stands proudly in front of her hand-painted tiles, along with our traveling buddy, Connie Roberson.

Gail Wilson

has graciously prepared a pizza feast tonight in her beautiful Italian kitchen. It was love at first sight, too, when Gail saw these creamy white and blue colored tiles while on our tour in Southern Italy.

151

Fabulous Doors

and more found at the local markets in Italy and built in the beautiful East Texas villa of Stephanie and Ben Sargent.

Peggy Garmon's

Fabulous Home

sits majestically behind the Pine Curtain in East Texas and drips with Italian charm, not to mention the doors...

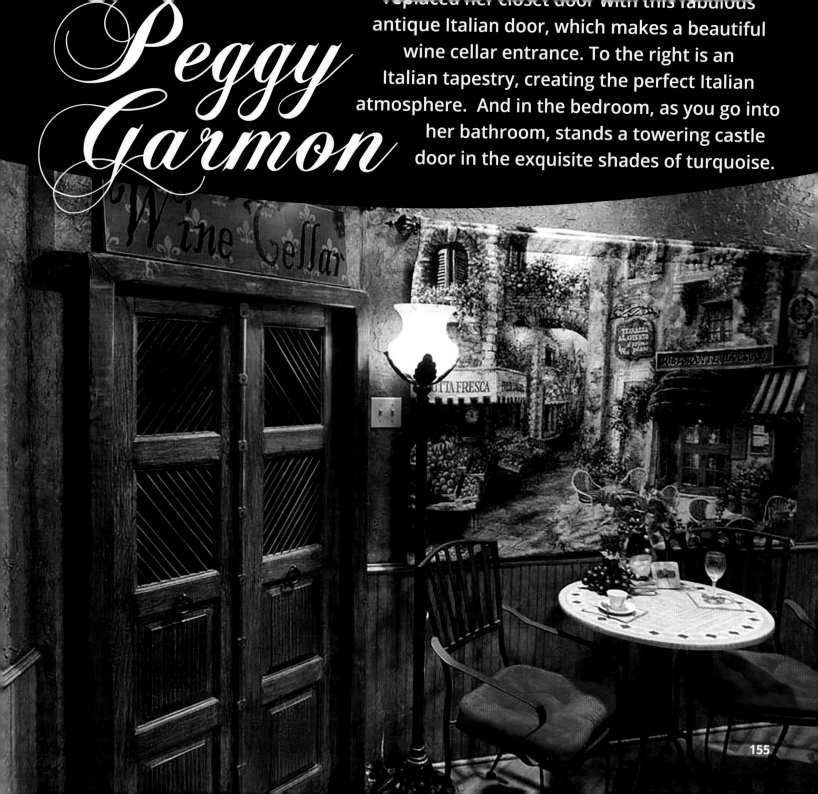

Peggy Garmon

...placed her closet door with this fabulous antique Italian door, which makes a beautiful wine cellar entrance. To the right is an Italian tapestry, creating the perfect Italian atmosphere. And in the bedroom, as you go into her bathroom, stands a towering castle door in the exquisite shades of turquoise.

159

In the home of

Gail
& Chuck
Wilson,

Peggy Garmon opens their fabulous, antique door with colorful stained glass windows. By using a little imagination, Gail decided to make it her hidden treasure chest.

Rose Jobe's

East Texas Home

is a treasure chest full of fabulous finds throughout Italy and beyond. This antique window with blue stained glass and an iron forged balcony is a rare find.

It's been my pleasure traveling Europe for Rose's beautiful home. Throughout the last sixteen years, I've shipped back for her stunning bronze statues, Carrara marble masterpieces, antique Blackamoors, Reliquaries of the most fabulous kind, and the list goes on and on. And, as of today, Rose has her eyes on a set of rare Watchmen that I found in Sicily.

My *Home* is always changing...

As I roam through local markets in Italy and other countries, I'm always on the hunt for another Icon and Ex Voto. In fact, a few chapters back you saw my prayer chapel and the many treasures inside. Weeks before this book went to press, I returned from Italy and Greece with more Icons...and, of course, I had to put them in my prayer room.

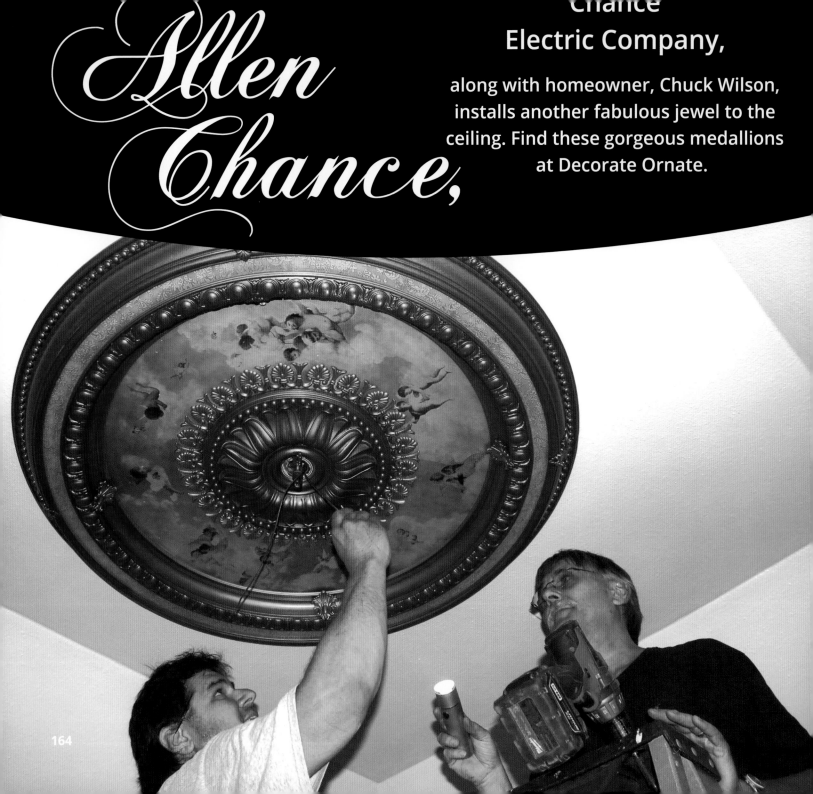

Allen Chance,

Chance
Electric Company, along with homeowner, Chuck Wilson, installs another fabulous jewel to the ceiling. Find these gorgeous medallions at Decorate Ornate.

164

Dee Tullis

adds another heirloom treasure to her fabulous East Texas ranch. This medallion—an artistry of angels—feels as though you've just entered the Sistine Chapel. Secured tightly to her dining room ceiling, it creates a soft detonation of renaissance elegance of the most fabulous kind while showcasing the stunning, antique chandelier dancing inches below.

> **Searching for treasures is a *Passion***
>
> I can never leave well enough alone. There is always a treasure to find and a creation to be made. My home will never be finished. It's my playhouse—growing and changing all the time with the things I love."
>
> ~ Stephanie Chance

We're at the local market in

Arezzo, Italy,

this morning and look what Tony and Nino find—a rare, silver icon, which I ship back to the USA for the perfect place—my prayer room. And before I take another two steps, I find this fabulous bedspread, which now adorns the Queen's chair.

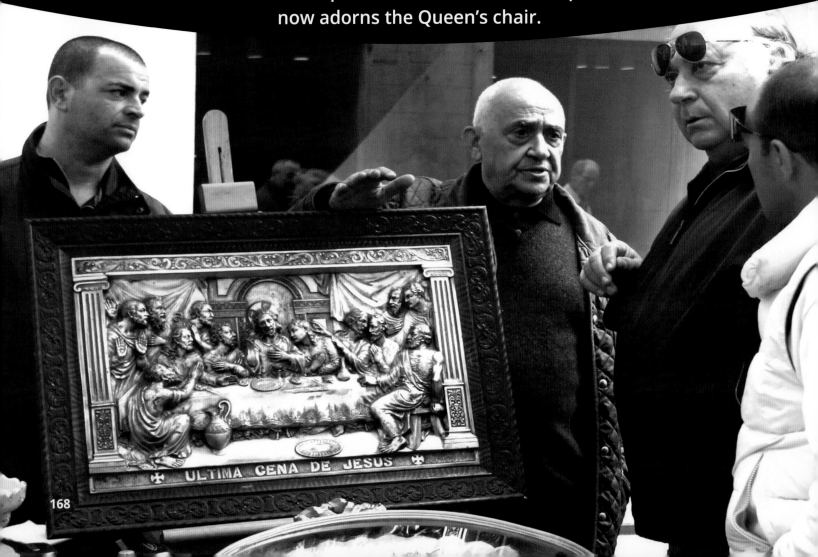

Home Sweet Home

Oh how I love this fairy-tale village. Twice a year I'm tucked away here. As I walk through the gates of this medieval, walled city—home of Saint Francis of Assisi—my heart beats rapidly at the sight of the painted mural on the local resident's home. Come on, follow along and see.

SANTA·MARIA·MADRE·DI·DIO·PREGA
PER·NOI·PECCATORI·ADESSO·E·NEL
L'ORA·DELLA·NOSTRA·MORTE·

173

Assisi, Italy, the crowning *Jewel* of Umbria... I love the peacefulness here.

179

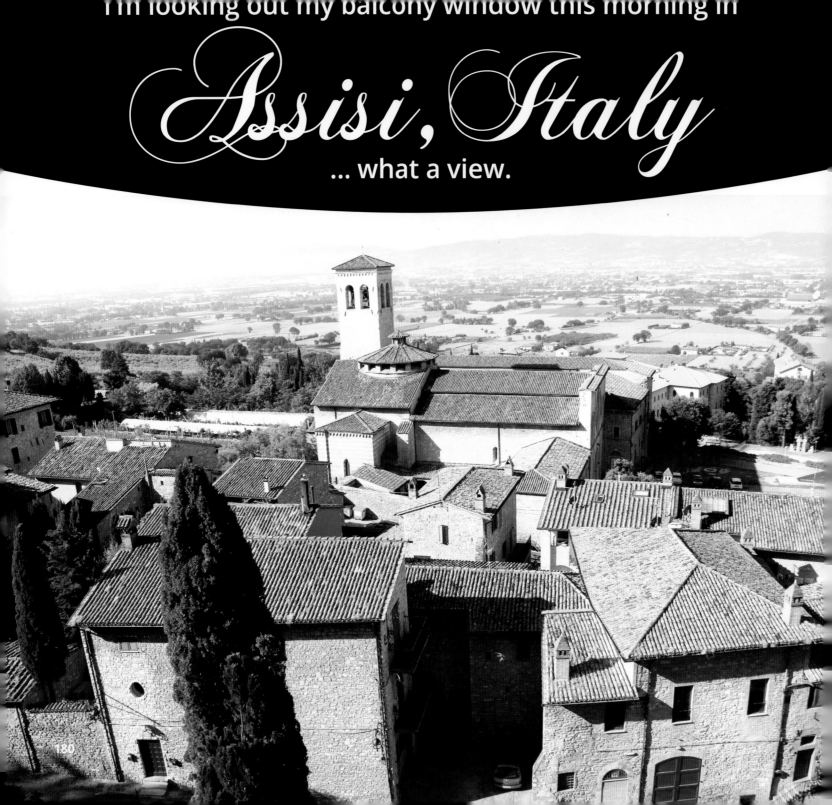

I'm looking out my balcony window this morning in

Assisi, Italy

... what a view.

181

Presepe, a *Nativity*

This morning we meet our friend from Napoli, Italy who brings the Presepe to Arezzo to sell. Napoli is famous for the Presepe. When including Napoli on my Italy tours, I love taking the Americans to the colorful shops tucked away on Via San Gregorio Armeno Street.

antique  *Presepe* sits proudly in the center of my fireplace mantel.

183

The early bird gets the worm... and this

Medieval Door

is going back to Decorate Ornate, along with a few more treasures that will end up in my home, for sure.

Hunting
in
Italy...

The artful blend of antiques I collect for my chapel is a passion within my soul. It's about my faith and the things I grew up with.   I'm drawn to ecclesiastical art.

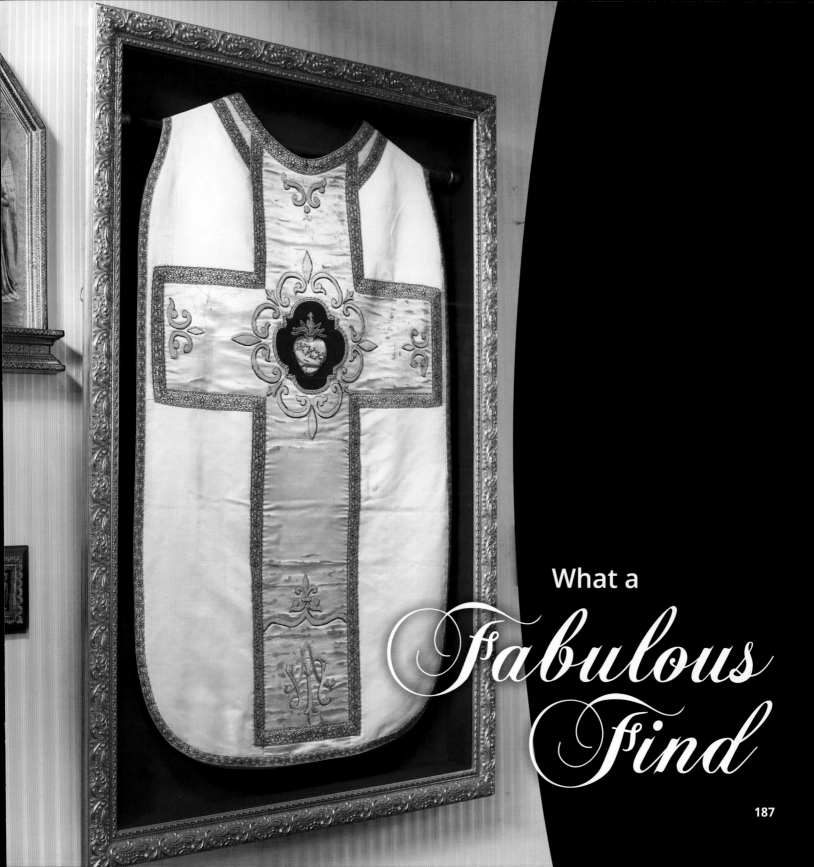

What a

Fabulous

Find

The *Joy* of finding treasures in Italy!

I love antique crowns, bronze statues & blackamoors... decorate with the things you love.

From *Italy* to my home.

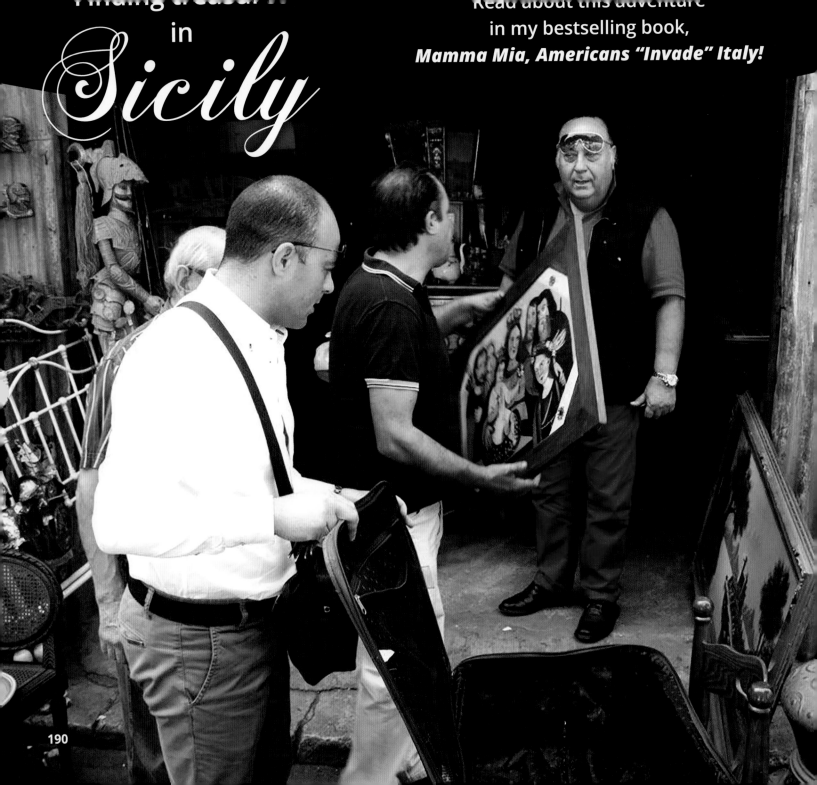

Finding treasure in *Sicily*

Read about this adventure in my bestselling book, *Mamma Mia, Americans "Invade" Italy!*

The joy of
finding
treasures for

My

Home

—how many
do you see?

Southern Italy

brings many surprises and many new friends from afar.

Please be
my
Valentine ...

194

Tony & Pat arrive from Italy... let the Valentine fun begin!

Create the
element
of *Surprise*
for your little
ones and guests.

Baci...

kiss me!

Baci per te

Create a
Wow!
entrance.

In the bed of roses stands a fabulous 4 foot, bronze

Candelabra

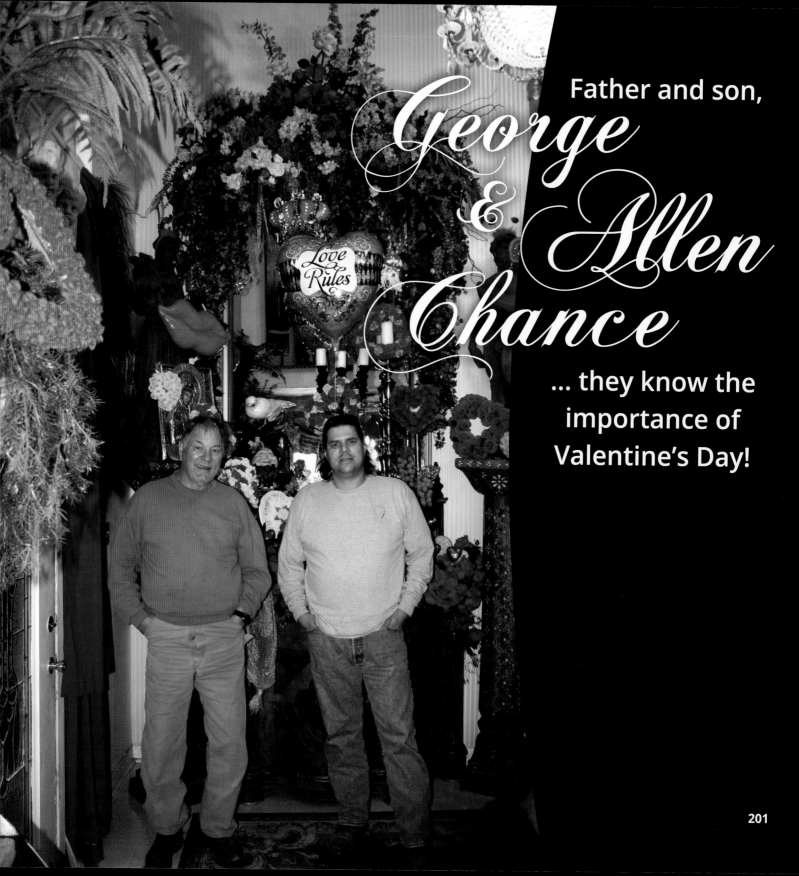

Father and son,
George & Allen Chance

... they know the importance of Valentine's Day!

Love Rules

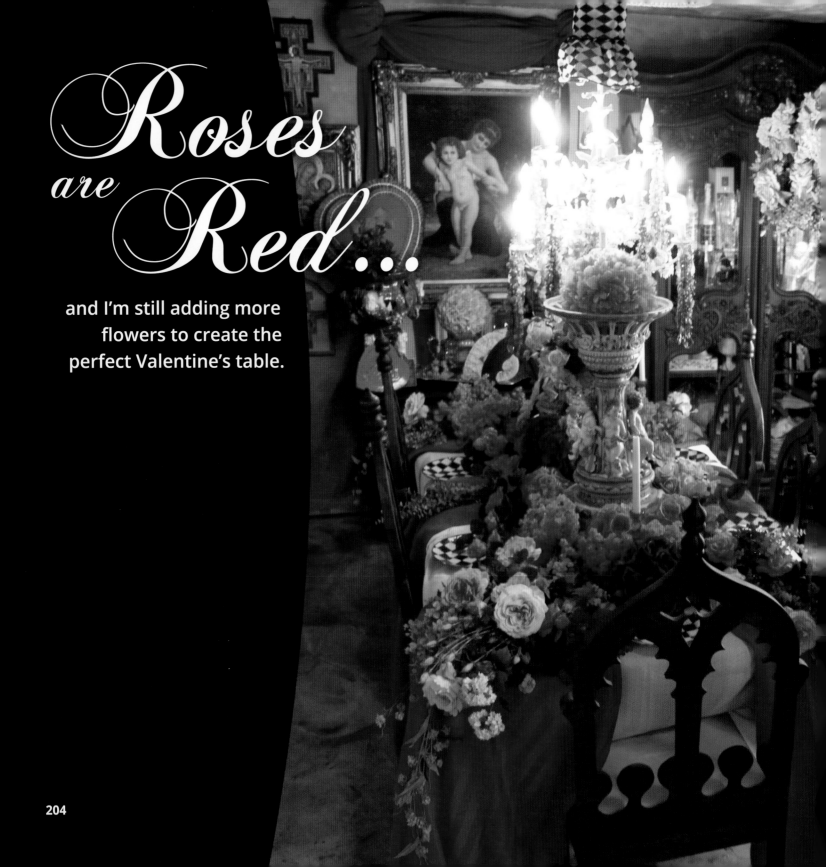

Roses are Red...

and I'm still adding more flowers to create the perfect Valentine's table.

204

Bring out the *Crystal...*

I love using my crystal glasses and oversized napkins. The napkins were found in Siena, Italy

For Valentine's Day, you can never have enough

Roses

With one stem at a time, create a seductive explosion of visual delights.

Dresden,
Germany

Compotes ...

still on the table.

The
Orchestrated
Beauty
continues
by adding a few
more stems to
the corners of
the table...

Easter
Celebration

Kaitlyn helps me create another

Floral Beauty

adding one stem at a time.

Amy

meets the babies... Verona Valentine and Mia Maria enjoy their first Easter Sunday.

228

229

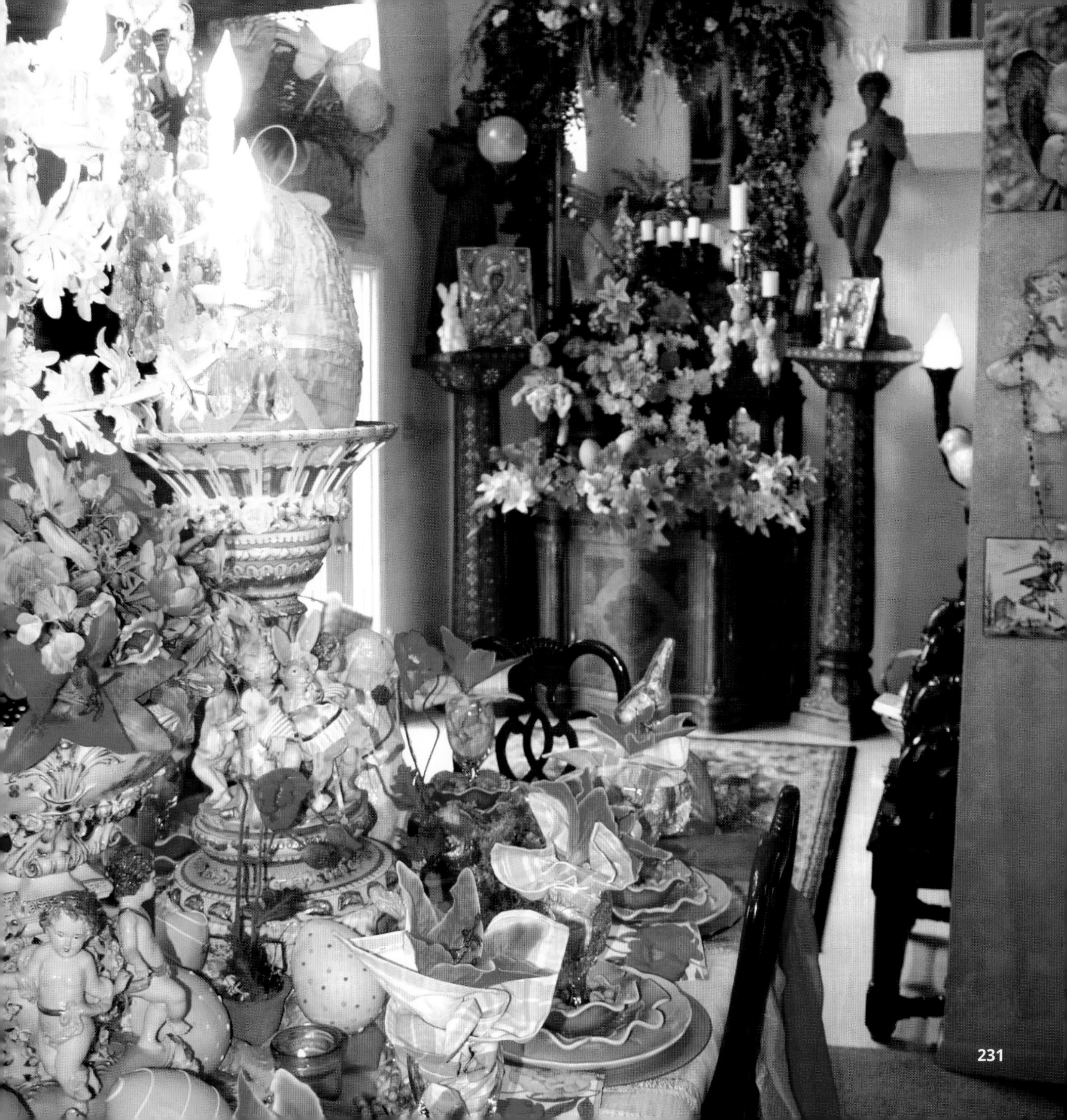

Kaitlyn's favorite *Easter Treat* a marshmallow Peep... so this gigantic Peep made the grand entrance.

Mix & Match

your dinner
plates.

Allow your little
ones to be

Creative...

Kaitlyn makes
Easter cards
for everyone...

241

And she always
makes the
Punch

Give me sugar,
vanilla, butter,
and lots of
Color

I am obsessed
with
Chocolate

...and, I love adding cut flowers and rose buds to my cakes. However, make sure you are using edible flowers, raised without harmful pesticides. If you're in a hurry to get your cake on the table, then purchase beautiful silk flowers. I love to add 'crystallized' flowers - covered in sugar. Whatever you do, make it fabulous and beautiful.

Remember, you are creating 'memories' for a lifetime!

Amy makes the annual
Piñata

Easter Sunday is a huge celebration in our home. It's a family tradition to gather after church for a meal; afterwards, Amy and Shane eagerly bring the piñata. Amy surprises us every year with a different creation she has made.

The Italian Riviera

Ah, the beautiful, turquoise blue sea, the famous Mediterranean that so many dream of, it splashes below the little hide-away beach houses on this remote island. It dangles by a thread from the mainland of Tuscany. Stretched across this secluded, celebrity property, are many cottages surrounded by hundreds of plants and flowers. We stroll through the arched veranda and groves of tropical trees and flowers, bypassing the ceramic-tiled swimming pool and

walking underneath
a huge cupola
with four gigantic
Corinthian columns,
to a grand villa
adorned with Pat's
English-Welch touch
and Tony's Sicilian love
for rare antiques. Ten
minutes from here,
zigzagging around the
edge of the crystal-clear
Mediterranean, is their
beloved daughter's two-
story villa, appearing
as though a famous
artist painted it into
being. Red poppies
dance amongst the
picturesque setting in
Giada's backyard as
a little church peeks
up from below and
the Mediterranean
Sea slaps the sand,
splashing hard
against the salted
shore.

Give me *Venice, Italy!*

Saint Mark's

Basilica

Home of the Apostle Mark
who is buried inside.

While strolling along the alleyways in Venice,
I wander inside another breathtaking church and behold
this beautiful silver and gold *Icon*

B. BOCCACCINO
(1467 - 1525)

Fabulously

hand-woven in Venice, Italy, and now in my home.

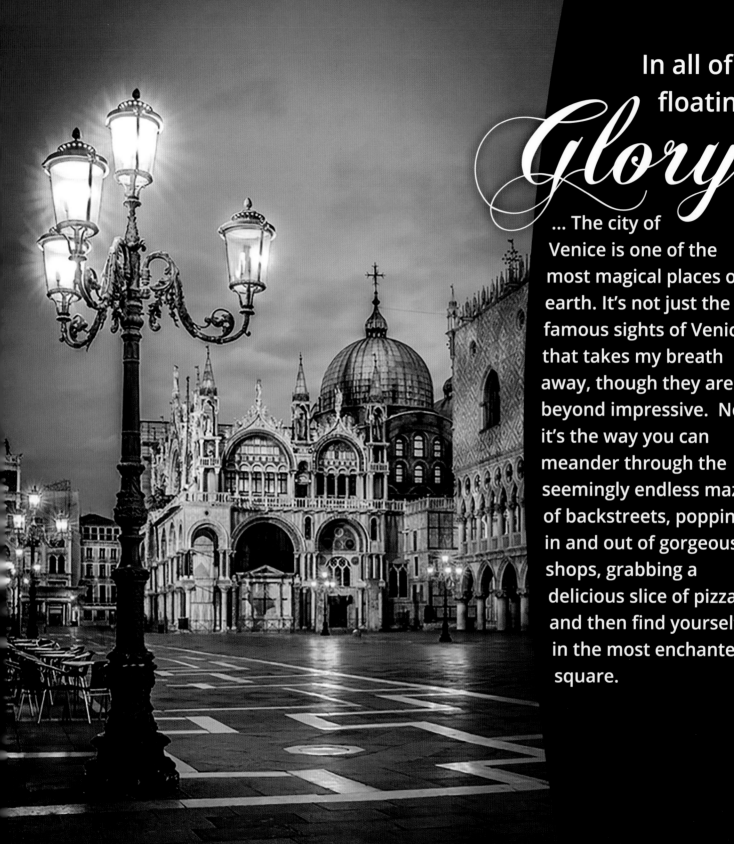

In all of its floating *Glory*

... The city of Venice is one of the most magical places on earth. It's not just the famous sights of Venice that takes my breath away, though they are beyond impressive. No, it's the way you can meander through the seemingly endless maze of backstreets, popping in and out of gorgeous shops, grabbing a delicious slice of pizza, and then find yourself in the most enchanted square.

The wall of *Collections*

—Guest powder room.

The Carnevale di Venezia showcases in the powder room, along with framed coral from the Mediterranean.

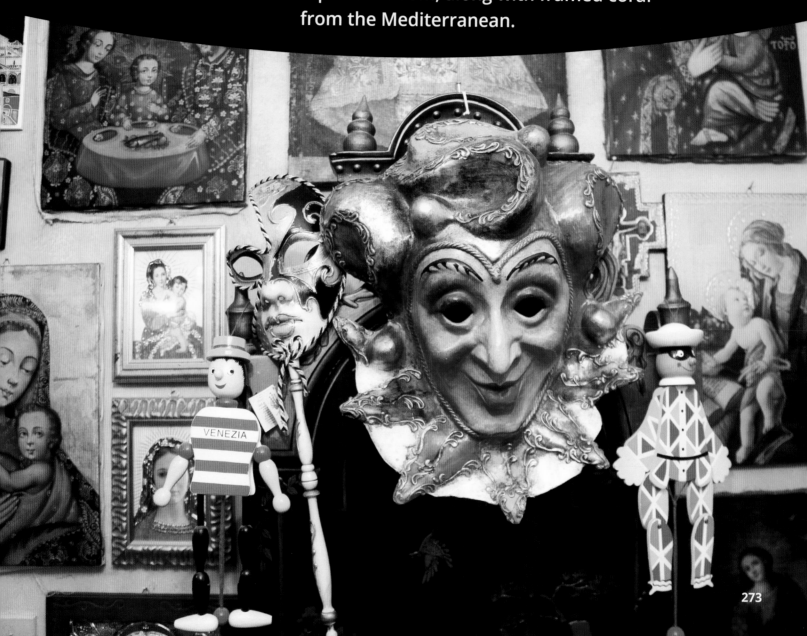

Guest

Powder Room

This wall of art comes from all over Italy. I love the Madonna...the Virgin Mary, the Mother of Jesus. To be a mother is God's greatest gift and deepest challenge. I am blessed with two children, a son, Shane and a daughter, Naiches.

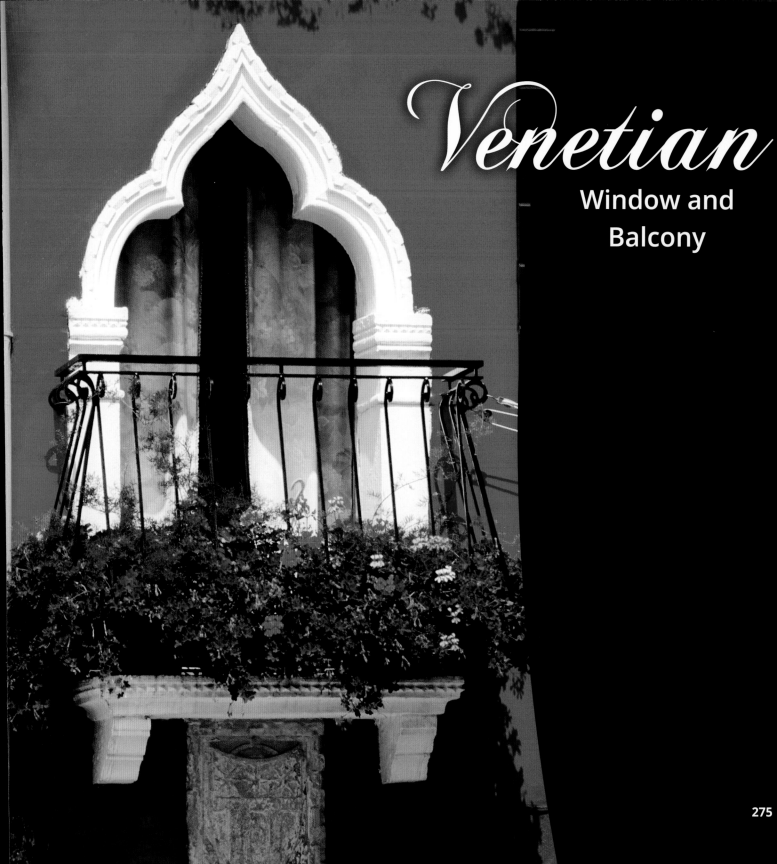

Venetian
Window and
Balcony

In Italy,
everywhere
we go,
Madonna
is near...

My love,
the
Shrines
throughout Italy.

The Cathedral of Saint Andrew is home of the Apostle Andrew in the Bible. A long flight of steps lead to a world of long ago, and looking from below is a visual treasure chest bursting out in divine glory. I love the beautiful pattern of Moorish arches and marble columns. The stunning biblical scenes depicting Jesus Christ and Saint Andrew the Apostle is truly amazing. The added bonus that calls out to me is the belfray decorated with coloured maiolica and crossed with arched friezes, not to mention the tympanum with mosaic by Domenico Morelli.

Sicily...
the Last
Harvest of
the Grapes—
at home with
Mimmo & Giusy.
Hop aboard
with us.

Marionette
Show in Sicily

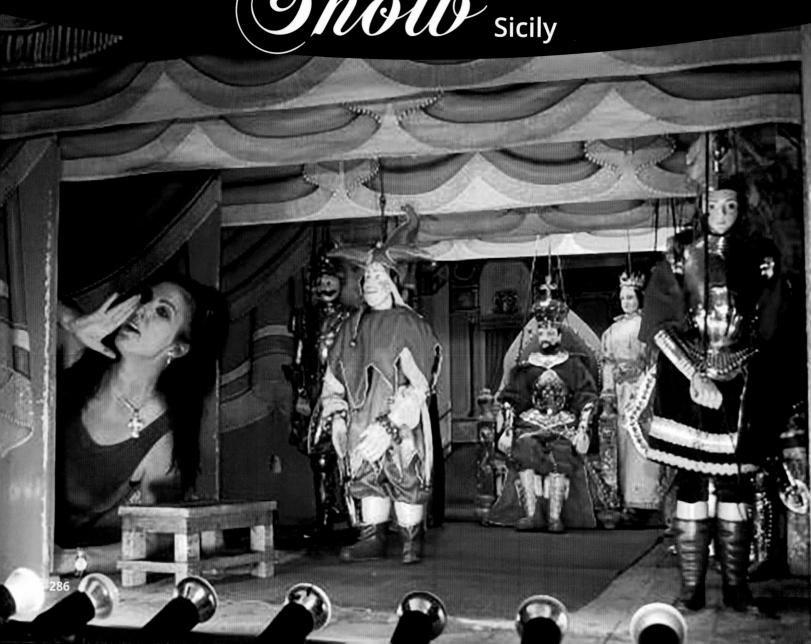

" It was *Love* at first sight," says Sandra Crow, who is in Sicily with Decorate Ornate Italy Tours.

Garry Steinbach shops Decorate Ornate. This fabulous *Trunk* was found in Italy but made in Damascus.

287

So many *Magical* places we go...

288

It's

Party Time

with the family...

Halloween...

the fun starts with my son, Shane, bringing me fresh flowers for my birthday, which is November 1, along with the sizzling aroma of Texas chili, slowly cooking on my stovetop. And only a few steps inside, the whimsical excitement of Halloween is in full motion as the shimmering colors create the magical ambience of spooky fun.

Every year,
Shane and Amy
surprise me with
their selection of
costumes, and if
I included them
all, it would take
another book.
Here are a few
of them. Enjoy

Pirates
of Villa Barboncini...

casa di barboncini
meaning,
House of Poodles.

Not only Shane, but Allen joins in with the *Fun*

297

Forever Memories...

The music is flowing, the chili is ready, and the spooky fun is exploding throughout the house.

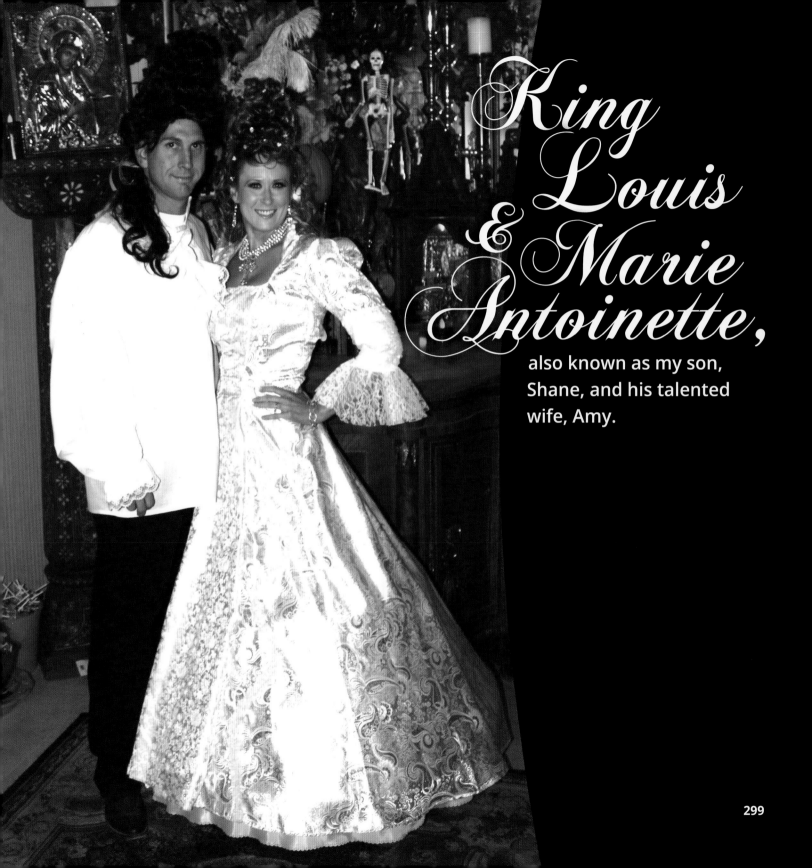

King Louis & Marie Antoinette,

also known as my son, Shane, and his talented wife, Amy.

299

Spooky Fun

Don't forget to dim the lights and start the music...within an hour or so, this entrance will be finished. The lights will be dimmed and the flickering candles will create the perfect spooky evening.

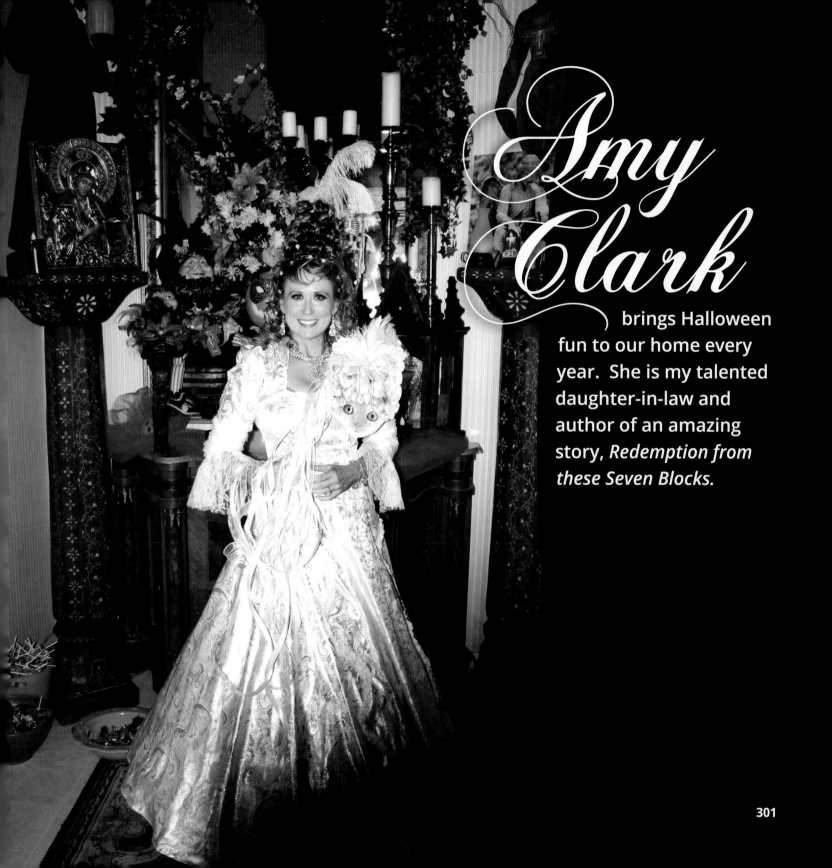

Amy Clark

brings Halloween fun to our home every year. She is my talented daughter-in-law and author of an amazing story, *Redemption from these Seven Blocks.*

The "Monster Mash" is echoing throughout the house as I prepare the kitchen with

Colorful Treats

The
Pumpkin Punch Bowl

waits to be filled as I eagerly decorate with colorful cookies, cupcakes, and a fun variety of spooky cakes.

Baby Shower Fun...

Oh how I love to create something out of the ordinary. And when it comes to needing an 'over-the-top' cake, I call the expert, Debbie Fontaine, owner of Edible Art in Longview, Texas.

Make the
Baby Shower
Spectacular
for your
loved ones..

It was an honor to give Aleesa & Shawn Hill a magical Baby Shower. I love to bring in the 'Wow" by starting with a fabulous cake. Not just one cake, but three to create drama. And to me, the chandelier is just as important...don't forget to decorate it. I love to create an explosion of color with my chandelier - it adds so much to the decor.

Bridal Shower...

This cake is designed by Stephanie Chance and the fabulous 'Chapel Cake' is designed by Debbie Fontaine of 'Edible Art Specialty Cakes & Cookies' in Longview, Texas.

Bridal Shower
Brooke - Joseph
This I Do, Love You!
June 26, 2005

I love
making

Bridal
Bouquets

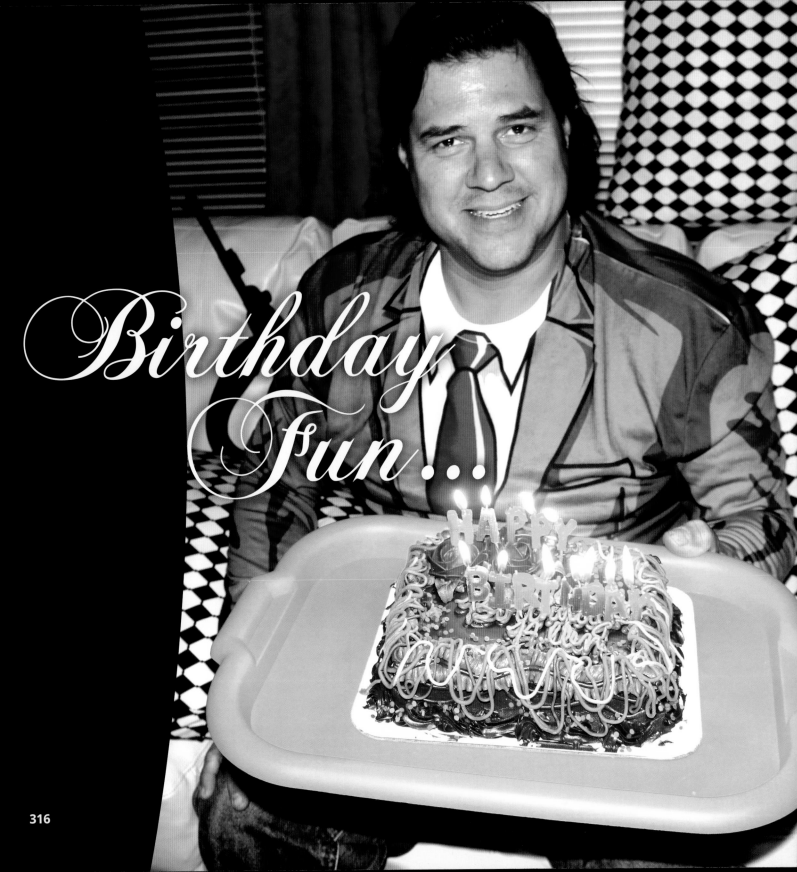

Birthday Fun...

I love
adding

Flowers

to my
cakes...

Love Italian
Style – Happy
Birthday,
Garry!

Happy
Birthday
Italian
Style

Baking... make it pretty!

Designing

Poodle Snacks

is so much fun...

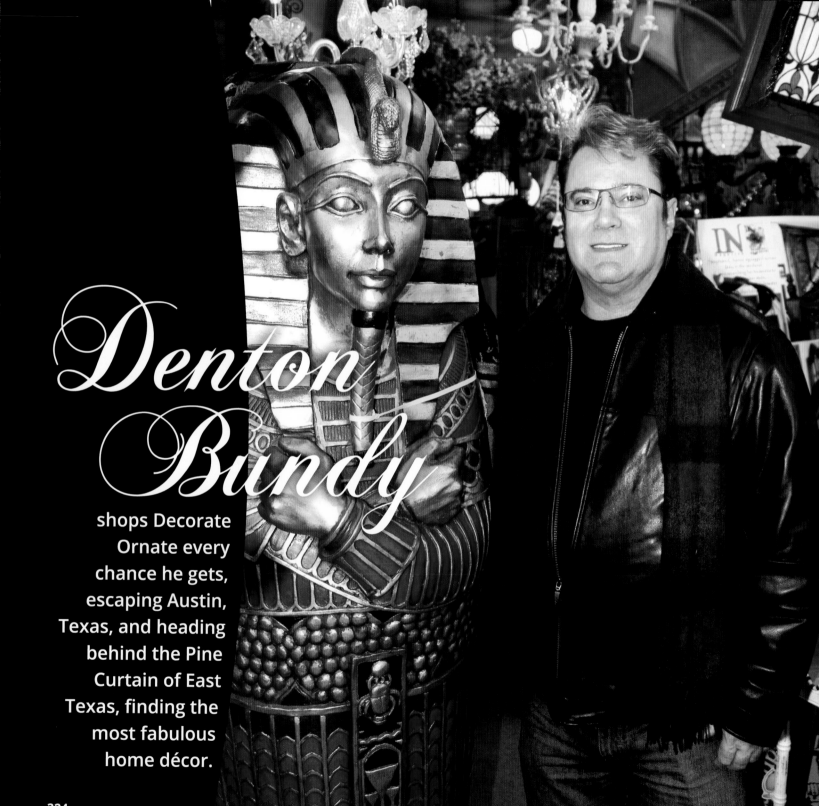

Denton Bundy

shops Decorate Ornate every chance he gets, escaping Austin, Texas, and heading behind the Pine Curtain of East Texas, finding the most fabulous home décor.

Exotic Meals

In his gourmet kitchen in Austin, Texas, Denton Bundy loves preparing

... such as his new American chic, which is fabulous for holiday dinner parties. Roasted pork tenderloin in a shiitake, demi-glace atop saffron rice with orange-ginger carrots, and topping it off with a Japanese eggplant sauté.

The love of *Decorating*

whether it's shoes, bags, glasses, hats, your furry animals, or your home, decorating is fun. Come along and see the many ways to decorate YOURSELF, such as murder mystery parties, target shooting in Texas, to visiting royalty in Italy, it's all about decorating and looking fabulous, whatever you're doing.

Murder Mystery Fun

COLLENE CANDY
CALL GIRL - TROYA

Dinner and a Party

Target Shooting

– born and raised in Texas.

Visiting
The Count
in Italy. Italians love
color and fashion.

330

Queen of Style...

Kathy Murphy

is the creator of the world's largest book club in the world
and author of *The Pulpwood Queens' Tiara Wearing, Book-Sharing Guide*

Live life to the fullest, but never forget the

Red Lips

When you go to Italy
with me, you will understand the red lips.

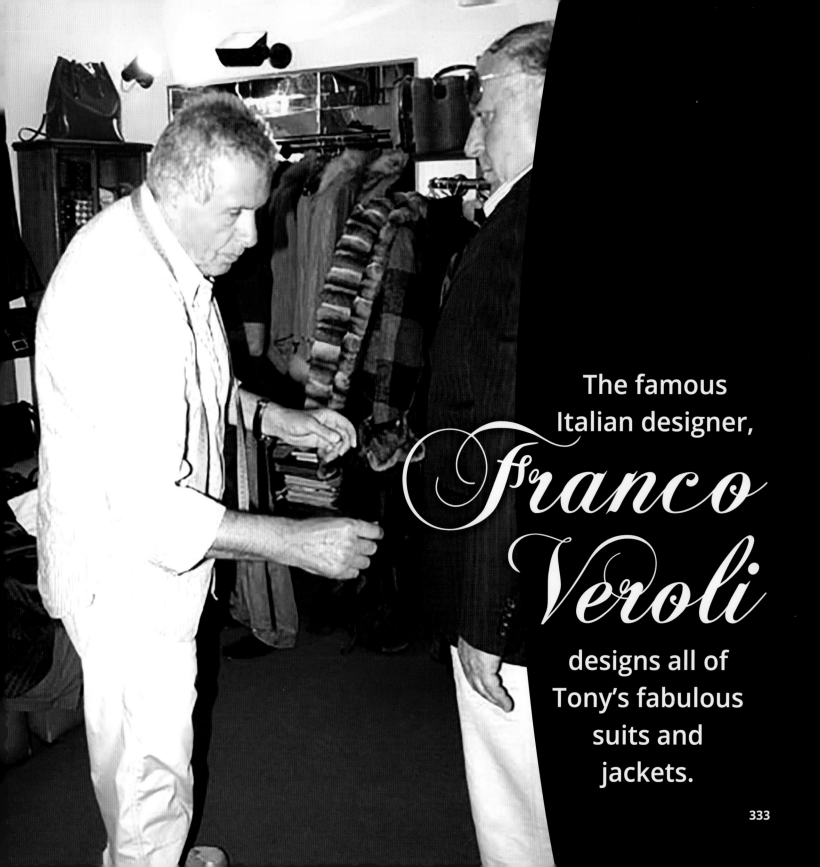

The famous
Italian designer,
*Franco
Veroli*
designs all of
Tony's fabulous
suits and
jackets.

Tony Franza's diva, *Zsa Zsa* is taking a moment to herself, lounging on her throne...

... and Mavi Vaselli's girl, *Katy* is relaxing and enjoying the breeze by the pool—both taking a break from shooting the pages of **"Scenes from the Life of a Glamorous Poodle."**

The beauty
of
Decorating...
make it
fabulous!

In life, whether we know it or not, we are always decorating. This is the backyard of my dear friend Tony Franza, a New York native and Master Stylist for the celebrities in the Hollywood hair industry for over three decades. We both share a huge love for poodles and color!

337

It's been fun sharing a glimpse into my world of decorating, along with friends and family. I would love to hear from you. You can correspond with me via email at ALNCHANCE@AOL.COM; on Facebook pages Stephanie Chance and/or Decorate Ornate and, of course, see all of the fabulous treasures arriving at Decorate Ornate via my website: DecorateOrnate.com.

If you love to travel, hop aboard with us to Italy and beyond, twice a year, on our magical, fairy-tale adventures. And, too, read about the true and hair-raising adventures of the Americans in Italy on our tours in my best-selling book *Mamma Mia, Americans "Invade" Italy!*

I hope you've enjoyed my thick, little book as much as I've enjoyed writing it for you. It gives me great pleasure to share my life and hopefully inspire you to make all things beautiful. I hope you remember to make your home your castle...be the Queen of your castle and buy the things you truly love.

If you ever find yourself behind the Pine Curtains of East Texas, please drop by and say hello at Decorate Ornate in Gladewater, Texas. And, if you want to experience the magical, fairy-tale adventures in Italy and beyond, then hop aboard with me on my annual May and September tours.

This book is available worldwide for retail/wholesale orders via:
Verona Valentino Editoria (Italy)

Available in USA at local bookstores and

@ Decorate Ornate
202 S. Main Street
Gladewater, Texas 75647 (USA)

Email: ALNCHANCE@AOL.COM

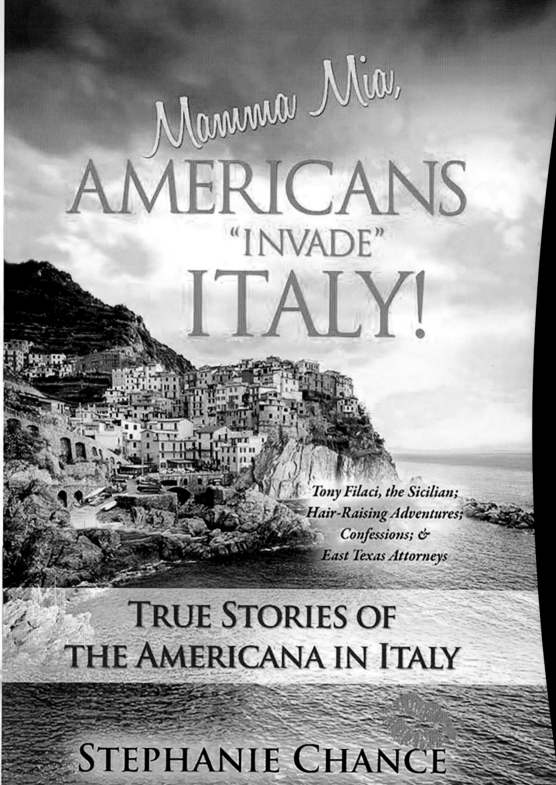

Mamma Mia,

AMERICANS
"INVADE"
ITALY!

Tony Filaci, the Sicilian;
Hair-Raising Adventures;
Confessions; &
East Texas Attorneys

TRUE STORIES OF
THE AMERICANA IN ITALY

STEPHANIE CHANCE